Beyond Waiting

Redefining the Purpose of Singleness

Rebekah Snyder

ANM publishers

Beyond Waiting

ISBN: 978-0-9715346-7-4 Paperback

Published by:

ANM
publishers

Advancing Native Missions
P.O. Box 5303 • Charlottesville, VA 22905
www.AdvancingNativeMissions.com

Dedication

To the man I will one day marry:
*When you've finished slaying your dragons,
you can come and find me here. I'll be the
one who isn't merely waiting.*

And...

*To the God who interrupts, redirects, and
fulfills my wildest dreams: Life with You has
been a most wonderful fairytale.*

Contents

INTRODUCTION: *Writing Your Story* 7

Chapter 1   *Do Something... Anything!* 17

Chapter 2   *Don't Slow Down; Make Him Catch Up* 33

Chapter 3   *Stop Searching, Sweetheart; Your Prince is Here* 49

Chapter 4   *The Things Only God Knows.* 67

Chapter 5   *Be Prepared... to be Used for God's Glory.* 85

Chapter 6   *Single by Choice.* 103

Chapter 7   *Start a Revolution: Learn to Love.* 121

Chapter 8   *The Search for Significance.* 137

CONCLUSION: *Happily Ever After* 155

An Introduction to the Palace. 161

Study Guide. 165

Acknowledgments 183

INTRODUCTION

Writing Your Story

"Enjoy the little things in life... For one day, you will look back and realize they were the big things."

-Robert Brault

Once upon a time, there was a young maiden who wanted nothing more than for her prince to come and sweep her off her feet. She sat at the windowsill, day after day, and dreamed of the moment of his arrival. She could envision the encounter in her mind. He would appear suddenly, riding over the ridge on his white horse—dashing, daring and strong—the most attractive man she had ever seen, without a doubt. With his dark hair, piercing blue eyes, and flawless smile, he would steal her heart within seconds… And so she waits.

Her friends come to her one sunny spring day and invite her to join them in their journey to the market. They'll look at all the lovely, new dresses shipped from afar, adorn themselves with exotic jewelry hand-crafted by natives, and breathe in the fragrant mixture of spices, perfumes, and delicacies from faraway ports. Afterwards, they will enjoy a picnic in the meadow and tell each other silly stories while they fashion daisy chains to braid into their hair.

"Oh, I can't come," the maiden wistfully replies. "I'm waiting for my prince."

The other young women run along on their adventure without her. She can hear their cheery laughter carrying across the rolling hills as they stroll down the pathway leading to the marketplace. But our heroine doesn't care. After all, she is waiting.

Summer sweeps in with its warmth and brightness, to find our young maiden still waiting near the windowsill. Again, the other girls appear and urge her to tag along on an outing to the forest. They plan to go swimming at the lake, then pick blackberries while they let their hair dry in the summer sun.

"I can't come today," the young woman insists. "I'm waiting for my prince."

The leaves turn brilliant shades of red and gold as summer fades to autumn. "We're preparing a large Harvest Festival with games and music and dancing. It is sure to be a wonderful time!" the village girls exclaim. "Please say that you will join us."

"I'm sorry, I can't. I'm waiting for my prince, you know."

Steadily, winter encroaches upon our young maiden as she closes the glass window panes to fight against the frosty chill. Yet never once does she allow her gaze to stray from the horizon. Eventually, a sharp rap sounds at her window. Is it her prince? Has the day finally arrived? But no, it is only the girls from town.

"We're going sledding," one young woman says. "And once our toes are completely frozen, we shall curl up by the fireside with mugs of hot cider. It will be positively delightful! Won't you come?"

"I can't go," the girl replies tiredly. "I'm waiting for my prince."

Again, the other girls leave her, and again, this young woman stares out the window wondering if this could be the day. The seasons continue to slip by, day after day, month after month, year after year. She has waited for so very long. Will he never come?

Finally, she notices a slight movement on the horizon. As the image draws closer, she realizes it is her prince. This is the man of her dreams. As he gallantly leaps from his horse and approaches her, she sees that he is everything she envisioned he would be.

"Where have you been?" she cries, rushing into his arms.

"Why, I've been training," he answers. "I've been honing my skills with the sword, practicing my jousting, fighting dragons and all number of ferocious beasts. I've spent days in the wilderness sleeping under the stars, sailed the seven seas with my comrades, and journeyed to distant lands. I've seen things that I never imagined existed. Why? What have you been doing?"

"Oh, I've been waiting…"

MOVING BEYOND WAITING

Perhaps that was a bit dramatic, and maybe a little overdone, but I cannot help feeling that this is the story many of us ladies are creating for ourselves. So much emphasis is put on dating and marriage in our culture. We boast slogans and sing songs declaring, "Someday My Prince Will Come." Well, that's great. I'm happy for you, truly. Maybe in five years he *will* come knocking at your door. But my question is, "What are you going to be doing in the meantime, while your prince is off fighting dragons?"

I think we would all agree that we would not want to read a three-hundred page novel about the young maiden in the preceding story. Six-hundred words was quite enough, thank you. Why? Because there is nothing thrilling or enticing about waiting.

Wait. It's a word we learn when we are very young, and one that we are repeatedly told throughout the course of our lives. "It will come. Just *wait.*" How frustrating those words are. Worse yet are the words, "You just *wait* until your father gets home!" That statement is enough to strike terror into the hearts of many a child. It's no wonder that the word *wait* carries such a negative connotation.

So what is the actual meaning of the word? I'm so glad you asked. According to the *Encarta World English Dictionary*, it can mean any of the following seven things:

1) Do nothing expecting something to happen

2) Stop so somebody can catch up

3) To be hoping for something or on the lookout for something

4) To be delayed or ignored for now

5) Be ready or available for someone to take or use

6) Delay something

7) Be a waiter

I don't know about you, but none of those definitions sound very appealing to me. In fact, the only one that comes even semi-close to what I think waiting should be is "to be ready or available"—if only there wasn't that nasty "for someone to take or use" tagged on the end. That sort of turned me off. When I first looked at this list, the thought that came to mind was, "That's what *waiting* is? It's no wonder we aren't content to be single." And that is when I fully decided that I was done with waiting.

I've decided that I don't want my life to be the story of the young maiden at the beginning of this book. In fact, I want my life story to be one that would be entertaining enough to turn into a novel. I want to go on grand adventures, sail the seven seas, and do things most people will never do in their entire lives. After all, those are the stories we read about in books.

You will most likely agree with me when I say that the heroines of our favorite stories are the maidens who have a dream and will stop at nothing until they achieve it. In stories such as these, you will notice that the leading lady actually becomes exasperated at the irritating man who keeps showing up and complicating things. Why is this? Because this man is not even on her radar. She isn't searching for Prince Charming; she is pursuing the goal that is set in her mind, the dream that beats in her heart.

I'm convinced that the fact that she is *not* looking makes it that much more romantic when Mr. Right does come along and sweep her off her feet. Don't you just love it when she looks into the eyes of her beloved and says, "I never dreamed…" And he replies, "Neither did I." Ah, now *there* is life. There is adventure. And somehow you know that this is right. This is how it was really meant to be.

In the chapters to follow, we are going to explore the seven definitions of waiting. And hopefully, in the process, we are going to break the chains that bind us to our own "windowsill" existence as we discover ways to turn our story into the one we would want to read—that of the girl who isn't merely waiting.

In a manner worthy of storybook heroines, I want to live my life so consumed with the calling that God has placed in my heart that I won't even notice when the right man comes along. Oh, he may be there in the background of my story, but I don't want him to come to the forefront until the day God finds that I am ready for him. On that day, I want God to have to tap me on the shoulder and say, "Hey, look over here. What do you think of so-and-so?" And I hope to reply, "What?" as if I had never even considered the possibility.

If you are finding that your story is all too similar to that of the maiden in our introduction, I want to challenge you to stop staring out at the horizon. Stop fantasizing that today might be the day. Instead, begin taking steps in the direction that will lead you beyond your *what-ifs*. Go on, take a stroll to the marketplace, enjoy a picnic with your friends, swim in the lake to your heart's content, and sip steaming cider by the fireside. You're waiting for your prince to find you anyway, so why not let him find you twirling in the middle of a dance floor, living life to its fullest? And when your prince finally does take you in his arms and asks you where you've been all his life, you'll have a better answer than, "Oh, I've been waiting…"

Chapter 1

Do Something...
Anything!

Waiting Defined:
Do Nothing Expecting Something
to Happen

*"The road to accomplishment is filled
with a lot of tempting parking places."*
-Bill Wilson

I recently went to the beach with my new friend Cathy. Although she lives only twenty minutes from the seashore, it took us nearly an hour to get there and find a parking space. Part of the reason that it took so long was because of the traffic we encountered along the way, but most of our delay occurred in the parking garage itself.

There was a lineup of about five cars all waiting for the departure of a young couple loading their car with their possessions and small child. We waited, and waited, and waited as this couple slowly prepared to leave. Since we were the second car in line, as we waited, we silently prayed that another space would open so we could park too.

Soon enough, a couple of guys appeared and started loading their truck. Then to our dismay, they began talking to the departing couple as if they were old friends who hadn't seen each other in years. When the couple finally pulled out, letting the car in front of us take their parking space, Cathy and I continued to wait for these two guys who were taking forever and a day to leave. In all honesty, I'm not sure what they were doing, but they kept pulling stuff out of the cab of their truck and loading it into the bed and vice versa. After five minutes of this "rearranging," we finally decided we were tired of waiting and drove on, hoping just to make the trek back down and find a different parking garage. Imagine our surprise when we pulled around the corner only to find over a dozen empty parking spaces just waiting to be occupied!

As we climbed out of the car, Cathy shared a profound insight on life. In her adorable Filipino accent, she explained, "We get so focused on this one space that we miss all the others." That statement left me pondering a new perspective on perspectives. I cannot help but wonder how often we do that with things in our lives. We focus our eyes on the one thing we *can* see, and end up missing out on the dozen other things that are still out of sight. If Cathy and I had realized what was waiting around the corner, we would not have wasted so much time just sitting there. Instead, we could have spent that extra half hour squishing our toes in the warm sand and letting the cool waves splash over our feet.

In similar manner, if you could just see around the corner to the glorious future God has in store for you, you might not waste your time dreaming about that guy you're crushing on right now. When I look back over my life, I can't help but laugh at my childish fantasies as I spent three years imagining myself in love with this one guy. He's married now, and as you've probably guessed, I'm not the woman who married him. But I have to laugh, because otherwise I would cry. I so wish I could take back those wasted years and do something worthwhile with them. The old adage rings true... if only I would have known then what I know now. If only I could have seen the *other* side of the fairytale.

"But this is different," you say. "This isn't just a childish crush; this really *is* love. He's everything I want in a husband, and I just know he's the one!" Maybe you're right, but even if he *is* the one God has for you, he's going to come to you in God's timing, whether you're waiting or not. So stop merely waiting, and do something with your life lest you end up like the girl from our opening story, who in truth, had no story to tell. The maiden from that story certainly knew our first definition of the word *wait*: *"Do nothing expecting something to happen."*

"But, Rebekah," you say, "I've always been told that the man is supposed to pursue the woman, not the other way around." I wholeheartedly agree with that statement, which is why I'm not implying that you leave waiting behind and begin relentlessly tracking down a husband. I will never ask you to pursue a man, but I will encourage you to pursue *yourself*.

MAKING A LIST AND CHECKING IT TWICE

If you've read any Christian books on dating or courting or waiting for Mr. Right, you've probably found that more than a few of them encourage you to make a list of the character traits you want in a husband. I personally found that when I wrote out a list of what I wanted my future husband to be, I started dwelling on him far too often. Perhaps it is the novelist in me, but when I wrote this man out on paper, he became real... and he was all I thought about. So I trashed my list and told God that I was just going to have to "know" when He was ready to bring Mr. Right into my life. While I still have a mental picture of the man I would someday like to marry, it is stashed in the back of my mind with all the other information I have stored for a different time and place.

As single women, we can spend too much time dreaming of who our future husband will be, yet not be nearly as concerned with the direction our own lives are taking. My question is: Shouldn't those things we desire in a husband be something we first strive to cultivate in ourselves?

> Contrary to what the world may insinuate when they refer to one's spouse as their "other half," God did not make you half a person.

Contrary to what the world may insinuate when they refer to one's spouse as their "other half," God did not make you half a person. You are a complete person with thoughts and dreams and your own, unique personality. And until you know who *you* are and what *you* want in life, I don't believe you are ready to look for someone who will live out those dreams alongside you.

I want to challenge you to make a list. (Hey, I figure if all those other authors can do it, so can I.) But I don't want you to write a list of attributes you would like in a husband. I want you to write a list of who you want to see *yourself* becoming over the next few months. List character traits you may struggle with, such as patience or humility, and resolve to intentionally work at overcoming or cultivating these things in your life, accordingly.

Next, I want you to work on your dreams. What is that one thing you've always wanted to do? It may be writing or dancing. Perhaps you've wanted to be able to run a marathon or play the piano better than Beethoven himself. I could spend all day listing things, but I'm willing to bet that your "one thing" has already popped into your mind. That one dream is tugging at your heart, begging to be released. I want to encourage you to set it free. Hone your writing skills, take piano lessons, get up and sing on the worship team at your church. Whatever your dream may be, take a step toward pursuing it. Then take another and another. Before you know it, you will have achieved it. Just don't forget to enjoy the adventure along the way.

Record your spiritual aspirations as well. This is the most important part of your list. Perhaps you want to read the Bible in one year or spend more time in prayer every day. Taking these small steps toward growing in Christ can make a significant difference in shaping and forming who you become as you yield yourself more fully to God's desires. As you spend more and more time at the feet of Jesus, you will not only gain a clearer understanding of Who *He* is, but you will simultaneously get a clearer picture of who *you* were truly meant to become.

Remain open to editing your list, since God may continue to reveal things to you as you grow and change. One day you will be able to look back and begin checking things off your list because you will have finally reached a goal, and before you know it, you will have reached another and another...

DISCOVERING YOU

I exchange letters with a teenage girl that I used to babysit. Shortly after I began working on this book, I received a letter from her that read:

Our last meeting for our Bible study was focused on using the years before you are married for God's glory, and not just moping around wishing your Prince Charming would rescue you. So, last night I was lying in bed thinking about how to use my single years for Christ. Then I realized that I should be using my talent for dance. It is a gift God has given me, and I must use it to gain as much as possible for His Kingdom.

She went on to share that although she had been invited several times to perform a dance at the church she attends, she continued to put off the opportunity as a "maybe later, if I have time" kind of thing. However, that evening she realized that dancing for church was a wonderful way to combine glorifying God and using her talents for God's Kingdom. She began to grasp that in choosing to go her own way and "put off" sharing her talent, she was, in reality, wasting some of the years that God was giving her to glorify Him *now*.

Having made the decision to perform a special dance, she was then faced with the next decision of which song to use. After a bit of struggle, the melody of a song began to enter her mind, but she couldn't recall the name of it. The next morning, she woke up and began her day without a thought of the "awakening" that she had experienced the previous night. As she prepared to run errands with her mom, she hopped into the car, and when the engine started, the radio began blaring a song. Her heart was instantly captured as she realized that it was the exact song that had been running through her mind the previous night. She immediately grabbed a pen and paper and wrote down the song title so that she could remember it and begin to work on her dance routine.

It thrills me to see a girl as young as thirteen recognize how God had called her to be used for His glory. Ariel knew that her passion for dancing had a purpose. If it was not meant to be used until her later years, then why did God give her the dream and ability when she was so young? I've seen Ariel dance, and it is absolutely breathtaking. When I watched the way she floated gracefully across the stage, I couldn't help but think, "She was made for this."

And so it is with you. It's time to find those dreams for which you were made. It's time to get to know yourself. Like Ariel said, your single life is supposed to be more than moping around

It's time to find those dreams for which you were made.

waiting on Prince Charming. So ask yourself questions like, "Who am I? What do I want to do with my life? If I only had a year left to live, what would I feel like I was missing if I never did it?" Ponder your passions. What makes you tick? If you had to give up all but one thing, which thing would you choose to hold on to for all you are worth? What causes you to think the things you do and feel the way you feel? And most importantly, what has God called you to do with all this?

I learn more about myself with every passing day. God has been bringing things to the surface of my heart that I never before knew existed. In this process of discovery, my dreams are changing as I'm pursuing one and being pulled toward another. Yet even though the dreams I once had are shifting, I'm not afraid of the change. I sense a stirring deep within, that God is somehow calling me toward something I don't want to miss. The more I delve into this new passion, the more I realize that it has been there all along; it was just buried under some different dreams. And I'm excited.

Don't be afraid of learning these new things. Get to know yourself; more importantly, get to like yourself. Become content with being who you are. As you begin to ask yourself questions, you will find that there are some things to which you don't know the answer, and that's okay. It's just a part of the journey—one more step in discovering yourself as you inch ever closer to becoming the person God intended you to be.

In response to your list, I also encourage you to keep a journal of the things you are learning about yourself. I have found that journals are an awesome way of remembering the things you would otherwise forget. So many of my own thoughts and spontaneous prayers would have been forgotten had I not written them down on paper. Throughout the years, I've been amazed to find that no matter how small the prayers, or how long ago they were prayed, God never forgets. He hears those prayers whispered in the silent darkness of our hearts, and He is faithful to answer each one.

THE OTHER SIDE OF THE FAIRYTALE

Ladies, there is a reason we are not born married, and it is not so we can spend our single years hunting for a man. It seems we are taught so much about waiting on God's timing and God's choice of a man, but we aren't told nearly enough to cherish our single years. In fact, the reason I began writing this book was because I was tired of reading other books that seemed to tell me, "Do this, in order to secure a better Christian husband." Personally, I believe there are better reasons to become a godly woman than just to marry a godly guy. But in our desperate quest to find a man and make him ours, we often forget to live these years to the fullest.

Let's face it, marriage changes things. It adds another person and responsibilities that have to be considered. A few weeks ago, for instance, a friend of mine got a phone call inviting her to join a friend for a trip to the beach the very next day. Since she did not have anything really pressing holding her back (like say, a husband and kids?), she went and had a wonderful time.

Now, before you misunderstand me and think that I'm against being married and having children, let me assure you that I am decidedly not. One of my greatest dreams is to get married and have a whole houseful of kids. I'm just trying to encourage you to not get so caught up in waiting for that special someone that you miss out on the exciting things happening in life. Those exciting things that are happening *now*. Don't mope around on Friday nights imagining that you are the only one without a date because that simply isn't true. There's always another girl who feels as lonely as you do, or better yet, there is that girl who plain old doesn't care that she is alone because she is content with her life as it is.

I've never dated anyone, and I don't feel as if I've missed anything… except for maybe a broken heart and a whole lot of tears. I've seen too many perfectly good friendships ruined by someone who tries to add romance to them. Not to mention, boyfriends take up an enormous amount of time. I've lost count of the number of times I've seen a friend start dating a guy, and suddenly, I don't see that friend anymore. To be honest with you, a relationship would cost valuable time that I really don't have to give right now. What little spare time I do have, I'm trying to devote to other dreams—bigger dreams.

That's right, I'm devoting my time to the *other* side of the fairytale. Exactly what is the other side of the fairytale, you ask? When I say the word "fairytale," you probably naturally think of Prince Charming and "happily ever after," but that isn't the entire fairytale. It's only the ending. For most of the story, the prince and fair lady are not even together. He's off fighting dragons, and she is trying to make something of her life.

Personally, I don't think Cinderella went to the ball to seduce the prince. I think she simply wanted to step outside her life of servitude, explore the inside of a palace for a day, and get lost in the wonder of music and dance. It was there that Prince Charming found her... and she rushed out on him because, believe it or not, he wasn't her primary concern. I believe we have distorted the fairytales. "Happily ever after" may be the ending, but the true romance, excitement, and adventure lie in the journey that leads to that ending. The real story, my friends, lies within the "Once upon a time... "

> *"Happily ever after" may be the ending, but the true romance, excitement, and adventure lie in the journey that leads to that ending.*

SECOND STAR TO THE RIGHT...

I had the most interesting conversation with a co-worker one morning. He was showing me a video of people holding an open-air church service in the rain.

"Well, it's not a bad rain," I injected. "That's the kind of rain that is perfect to dance in."

He sort of chuckled, shaking his head.

"What?" I asked. "You've never danced in the rain before?"

"Seems like a childish thing to do," he said.

"Well good," I replied. "I don't want to grow up. I'm running away to Never-Neverland. I'm going to dance in the rain and splash about with the mermaids."

"When are you leaving?" he questioned.

"Right now. Second star to the right and straight on 'til morning. Want to come?"

When he shook his head, I teased that he would most likely join the pirates and end up just like Captain Hook anyway, so it was probably for the best. After our jovial conversation, I walked away thinking that I never want to get too old to dance in the rain. I never want to tire of catching fireflies and splashing in the ocean waves. I always want to live with a childlike heart.

What I find so fascinating about children is that they are fascinated by everything—a blade of grass, a caterpillar that slowly inches its way across a sidewalk, or a storybook in which they still find something new and amazing even after the sixth time you read it. If I have learned anything from my years of babysitting and growing up among a myriad of young cousins, it is this: Anything can be an adventure as long as you allow it to captivate your very heart and soul.

So maybe you can't afford to go on some exotic cruise around the world, but you can go to the downtown mall and check out some of the cool scarves and jewelry that have been handcrafted in other countries. You may never sail the seven seas, but perhaps you can take a canoe trip down a river, or maybe your friend has a boat and you can go tubing in a nearby lake. And though Mt. Everest may remain forever out of sight, you can still climb that hill in your backyard and have fun rolling down it. You may get some weird looks from the people who don't understand such "childish" things (which is why it is always good to invite a close friend on these little excursions; at least you will be looking ridiculous together), but the opinions of others don't truly matter.

These things may seem trivial, but I hope you understand that I am merely challenging you to enjoy life—no matter how simply. I want you to learn to live before your life is over and you look back only to realize how many years you wasted in waiting. Don't get so focused on the "one space" that you miss all the others awaiting you just around the corner. After all, this story is not about *him*, but *you*. So don't just sit around *doing nothing expecting something to happen*; get out there and live. Pick up the pen and start writing your story. I'll even start it for you. "Once upon a time…"

Chapter 2

Don't Slow Down;
Make Him Catch Up

Waiting Defined:
Stop So Somebody Can Catch Up

> Don't sacrifice the big dreams, because
> you may have to sacrifice the small;
> and one day when you look back, you
> will have sacrificed them all.

I recently stumbled across an interview with Kristin Chenoweth where she said something along the lines of: "In this thing we call show business, is it easier to be a Christian or a recovering crack addict? Definitely a recovering crack addict... I'm kidding!"

But was she? I honestly believe her statement was not far from the truth. I once performed in a drama presentation with my youth group where I portrayed a model. There I was on Easter morning in a sexy little red dress doing my less-than-modest model walk across the stage. I felt completely exposed, and I don't think it was even the dress that made me feel so uncomfortable—although it was true that I didn't normally wear things that were quite so revealing. What really bothered me was the role I was playing. The short amount of time I portrayed that character seemed to stretch on for an eternity. I could not wait to get out of that dress and pretend the whole thing had never happened.

I received all kinds of comments that day, the only true compliment being, "You did a really good job, but that was *so* out of character!" When another friend walked up and told me I did a good job, I replied, "Don't tell me that."

"Well, what do you want me to tell you?" he asked. "'That was horrible, you can't act at all, you should give up on life?'"

"That would be preferable," I confessed.

"You are really strange," he said.

No, not strange, just ashamed.

Shame? Isn't that sort of a strong word to describe something that was all an act? I mean, it's not like I behave like that model in real life. It's almost like it wasn't me at all, right? I was simply portraying a completely different person. The key word there is "I." *I* was portraying a completely different person, but in essence, that person was still me.

I'll bet that when Sandra Bullock's best friends watch *Miss Congeniality*, they don't see Agent Grace Hart; they see Sandra Bullock. And so it was with me as I strutted across that familiar stage. The people who were making comments hadn't seen an immodest model, but Rebekah Snyder doing an immodest model walk, and it had floored them. I think most of those people didn't know what to say. After all, as an old family friend jokingly told my father that day, "How do you tell a man his daughter plays a good trollop?"

I returned the borrowed dress, thankful that I only had to spend five minutes instead of five months in that role. I can't imagine being a Christian in Hollywood. It is hard enough being a Christian in the rest of the world. What if you were cast in a role that you felt was completely ungodly? How would you respond to the constant hammering away at your convictions?

But I don't need Hollywood to tell me how easy it is to compromise. We've all done it. We find ourselves thinking things like, "I know these shorts are really short, but so-and-so wears them, and she's a Christian, so I can wear them too," or "Well, I know I still have homework to do, but Jill invited me to this party, so the homework can wait. It doesn't count for that much of my grade anyway, so even if I turn it in late, it won't really matter. And this party will be totally worth it."

Do not be deceived into thinking that compromising has to involve something that is considered sinful. Shortly before I sat down to write this chapter, I was considering compromising, myself. I knew God wanted me to work on this book this weekend, but there was a special worship service at church tonight, and I really would have preferred to attend it. I started thinking that I could make up for the lost time tomorrow, or the day after that, or the day after that, or... well, you get the point.

Compromise is easy—especially when it comes to the topic of men. In fact, men might be the key factor lying behind the compromises of things like "short shorts" and "Jill's party." We want so desperately to be noticed, appreciated, and loved. But instead of seeking that affirmation from God and the dreams He has given us, we tend to get sidetracked by the next guy who comes along.

"But God, he's really cute, and well, he *did* ask me out. One date won't hurt." And neither will the second or the third or... It's that whole cycle of compromise.

It's a downward spiral into which it is so easy to fall, but much harder to pull yourself out.

One day when I was trying to match a particular guy to my mental list of standards which I believed I wanted in a husband (That's right, I didn't always feel this way about relationships, and sometimes I have the occasional relapse), I bumped up against his dreams. It's not that his dreams weren't admirable; they just did not interest me in the least. I decided that those dreams weren't something I wanted to spend the rest of my life hearing about. Can you just imagine it? "So honey, how was work today?" Blah, blah, blah… I wasn't in the mood to compromise, so I found myself telling God, "If this relationship is meant to be, You're going to have to change his dreams because I'm sure not changing mine!" Then I caught myself. If *I'm* not willing to change my dreams for some guy, then why should I expect *him* to change his for me?

> If I'm not willing to change my dreams for some guy, then why should I expect him to change his for me?

I'll admit that I have some pretty big dreams. My first dream was to be a missionary. After graduating high school, I joined up with a missions organization that helps equip native missionaries in spreading the Gospel throughout the world. I guess you could say that makes me a missionary to missionaries. I also want to be a novelist. I've been telling stories all my life and they are dying to come out on paper. And while one of my greatest dreams is to be a wife and mother, I feel like that is one dream I cannot run after in this moment. Pursuing marriage takes a lot of time and effort, and I'm already feeling as if there are not enough hours in the day. I know in my heart that if I actively pursue the dream of marriage, I will overlook all the other dreams that have been in my heart for so long.

MISSIONARIES, AND PENCILS, AND PRINCES... OH MY!

When I read the words to our second definition of waiting, *"Stop so somebody can catch up,"* I was instantly transported back to a moment where I had heard words of a very similar kind. I was sitting on a kitchen barstool as my adopted brother Donald animatedly told me and my mom of his efforts to find a soul mate. He explained that life is a path everyone must walk in order to reach the place to which God has called them.

"This is me," he said, lifting a pencil from the island that stood between us. "This is where I started," he explained, motioning to one side of the countertop before pointing to the other side, "and that is where I am going." Guiding the pencil in a straight line, he began to explain how he would often get distracted when a young woman would cross his path because he would start imagining that she might be "the one." At this point, he picked up another pencil and brought it across the path of the first one. The first pencil veered off the invisible path in pursuit of the new pencil as Donald explained how he would often stray from the path that led to his dreams, while in pursuit of a prospective bride, only to come swerving back some time later when he realized she wasn't the one God had planned for him. Pencils flew back and forth across the countertop as Donald demonstrated how he would repeat this habit of searching until he was exhausted.

After all that searching, the only thing Donald found was that he had not moved any closer to his God-given goal because he had been walking sideways instead of forward. The pencils in his hands came to a standstill as Donald's voice grew more serious. As he set his pencil resolutely back on its imaginary path, slowly bouncing it toward the goal, it was obvious that he was about to share a secret he had learned. "The girl who is right for me," he began, "is not the one who will cross in front of me, leading me off my path. When God brings the right girl," he explained, drawing the pencil in his other hand close to the first, "she will come and run *alongside* me."

I don't know about you, but I'm fed up with the fact that I have not moved any closer to my dreams because I've been too busy veering off-course in search of a man. I'm sick of compromising. I'm tired of wasting my energy on the futile cause of trying to make some guy conform to my standards. What a relief it was to hear Donald say that I don't have to keep running after some mirage of Prince Charming. I don't have to slow down for a guy who is hauling all his baggage.

When the time is right, my prince will come and run *alongside* me.

My friend Carmen is a real inspiration to me. She was single for many years, and her marriage was a set-up to which she was opposed from the start. Carmen has traveled the world, and her work in missions was something that she wasn't willing to give up for anything or anyone. Long before she met her husband Dan she had told God that if He ever wanted her to get married, this man's passion for the country of her heart would have to rival her own. Mind you, she told me this story on a day that she and her husband had just received some super-exciting news from the mission field, and Dan was positively gushing. (I know "gushing" is not a word that is typically used to describe middle-aged men, but I call them like I see them, and that was definitely a "gush.") Dan was making his joy obvious to the world when Carmen glanced over her shoulder at me and said, "Be careful what you wish for."

I smiled at her playful jab, but in all honesty, I wouldn't mind having my story be similar to Dan and Carmen's. I think the most beautiful thing about their relationship is that they both had their own dreams fully established before their lives merged into one big, unified dream. I'm sure that when Carmen prayed that prayer, she never truly believed that she would find someone whose passion rivaled her own, but sure enough, along came Dan. And neither of them had to sacrifice their personal dreams, because their dreams were one. Carmen never veered off course, and Dan still caught her.

While our culture tends to view Prince Charming as the fulfillment of every young women's dream, I think we've got it all wrong. It's true that Prince C. may be the fulfillment of *one* dream, but I'm pretty sure you have other dreams as well. I know I do. Let me share something with you that will totally rock your fairytale-founded world: Your dreams are not meant for someone else to fulfill. If God had wanted someone else to write the book He has placed on *your* heart, play the music that flows from *your* fingertips, or teach those little second graders whom *you* have come to adore, He would have given those dreams to someone else. He would have given them to the person who *was* meant to fulfill them. The fact is, He did. You, my friend, are the only person who can accomplish those dreams, because you are the only one who has dared to dream them. But how often do we delay those dreams as we rush to chase after another? We think that if we are ever going to get married, we have to actively pursue *that* dream—we have to be constantly running after some guy in hopes that he's "the one."

Your dreams are not meant for someone else to fulfill.

DITCH THE SWOONING, SISTER. IT'S TIME TO PICK UP YOUR SWORD.

Having grown up near a woods with three brothers, I spent many childhood days tromping through downed timber and jumping from rock to rock in a creek. Let's just say from experience that it's hard to become a fair lady when your closest childhood companions are young knights in training. It was either keep up and climb trees with the best of them, or be left back at the house by myself. Naturally, I wouldn't develop into a swooning maiden. I'm more like a Joan of Arc who has never quite mastered the art of playing the role of "damsel in distress."

This dislike for playing "the pampered maiden" showed itself one day when I went boating with some friends. At the end of our excursion, one of the guys offered his hand to one of the other girls in an attempt to guide her safely from the boat onto the deck. She made the appropriate, nervous laughter as she cautiously extended her leg over the edge of the boat, allowing him to steady her as she grasped for solid ground. When that same guy reached for my hand, I simply stepped up onto the edge of the boat and jumped down onto the dock. He blinked a couple times before asking, "And why did I grab your hand?" I just shrugged and laughed as I continued on my way.

Those of you girly-girls may think I've taken this to the extreme, but I don't agree. It's not like I've lost every trace of femininity. I still wear dresses. I like looking pretty. I love the idea of having someone fight for me, but the time comes when one must awaken herself from her fairytale fantasies. And while I may dream of Prince Charming rushing to the rescue, there are still plenty of times I'll have to fight for myself. It's interesting to note that the fairytale damsel in distress is not found passively waiting for her knight to come save her. She is actively fighting against her captors and tearing at her ropes in a desperate attempt to be free.

In similar fashion, there are things that hold us captive—bonds that keep us from pursuing our dreams and embracing the wonder of living. We wait, as if for our knight to come rushing in so our story can begin, but once again, we are looking at the fairytale backwards. The prince does not enter the beginning scenes of the tale, but rather the ending. Until your prince comes riding in, you must learn to slay your own dragons. And even after your knight arrives, don't be deceived into thinking he can destroy all the beasts that lie in your past. I hate to break it to you, princess, but your knight is going to come complete with dragons of his own. While he may fight alongside you, he cannot be expected to defeat all the dragons that line the pathway of life.

> *Your dreams are something you have to be willing to fight for.*

Your dreams are something *you* have to be willing to fight for. You have to be ready to pursue them with everything that you are—with all the tenacity that is within you. When God gives you a vision, you run toward it, and you don't stop running until He tells you that you have gone far enough. You don't slow down. Ever. And you don't turn your head to the right or left, because you will be distracted if you do.

My co-workers are constantly trying to marry me off. One day, when one of them (remember Captain Hook?) informed me that he was trying to find me a husband, I responded, "Please don't."

"Well, why not?" he asked.

"Because I've got better things to do."

"What if Prince Charming comes knocking on your door tomorrow?" he challenged.

"I'd tell him to come back in two years," I replied without hesitating.

"Well, what if he doesn't want to wait two years?" the old pirate pressed.

"Then he's not my Prince Charming!" I adamantly declared. And I truly believe those words. My prince is not going to slow me down. He is not going to turn me away from the goal toward which God has called me.

John 10:10 tells us that Jesus came to give us life to the full. I don't believe this promise is one you must wait until after marriage to gain. Who ever decided that you must be married before life begins? I want you to do something with me. Close your eyes and dream that dream—that one thing that you want to do more than anything else in the world. Isn't it beautiful? Imagine the victory that will come when you finally obtain this one thing. It's so close you can almost taste it. You can nearly feel the triumph in the depths of your soul. That's it. Keep running. Don't slow down. Don't compromise. Don't surrender such a glorious dream in exchange for anyone. When the right guy comes along, he will not pull you away from your calling because he will understand why your heart pounds with excitement and your face lights up at the very thought of this dream. The right guy will know why you have to achieve it, and he will not only be your biggest cheerleader, he will run the whole road alongside you.

OVERCOMING THE DESTROYER OF DREAMS

The first thing Satan ever destroyed was a relationship. He ended his relationship with God when he decided he could take care of himself. Not only did He imagine himself to be better off without God, but he has been feeding that same lie to humankind ever since. By convincing Eve to eat the forbidden fruit, Satan severed her relationship with God, which greatly complicated the relationship between Eve and her husband. The second thing Satan crushed was a dream. When Satan talked Eve into taking a bite of the forbidden fruit, he brought an end to a dream— God's dream. And I'm sure Adam and Eve's dreams were destroyed, as well.

Just as Satan used relationships to destroy a dream back then, he is continuing to use them today. Perhaps it's the fact that beauty reminds him of what he lost in his rebellion, maybe that's why he insists on destroying the most beautiful things in life. Make no mistake about it, Satan is out to destroy your dreams and relationships. Indeed, he often uses one to thwart the other. Ephesians 6:12 says, "For our struggle is not against flesh and blood, but against the powers of this dark world and against the spiritual forces of evil in the heavenly realms." The dragon has risen from the depths of the earth and has determined to unleash his fury upon you.

But you must not allow yourself to be defeated. While the world may not understand you—may not feel the passion that has infused every molecule of your being—the dream is still there. Though others may laugh, you must keep running toward that dream that has captured your heart. Eventually, the day will come when you sense that you are no longer alone. On that day, you will turn your head and find that your prince is there, running alongside you. And then you must run even faster—just to see if he can keep up.

Chapter 3

Stop Searching, Sweetheart; Your Prince Is Here

Waiting Defined:
To be Hoping for Something or on the Lookout for Something

> "Don't instill, or allow anybody else to instill into the hearts of your girls the idea that marriage is the chief end of life. If you do, don't be surprised if they get engaged to the first empty, useless fool they come across."
>
> -William Booth

Have you ever seen the movie *Enchanted*? I think it's one of my favorites. Not only does it combine several fairytales into one, which is unusual enough, but it also contains something else that makes this fairytale a little unconventional. The opening scene is your stereotypical fairytale. The young maiden, Giselle, is fantasizing over this prince she had met in her dreams. The prince, Edward, is out troll-hunting when he hears her melodious voice singing about *True Love's Kiss*. He immediately joins in her song as he rides to meet her. The captured troll breaks loose, chases after our maiden, and eventually causes our heroine to land directly in her prince's arms. Prince Edward dramatically declares what may very well be my favorite line in the entire movie: "Ah, Giselle, we shall be married in the morning!" And they ride off into the sunset as they finish their duet.

Fast-forward to the wedding day—also typical fairytale-style. Suddenly, the evil queen appears in the form of an old woman who shoves Giselle down a wishing well, ultimately sending her to a place "where there are no 'happily ever afters'"—modern-day New York City. What first appears to be Giselle's worst nightmare turns out, instead, to be the fulfillment of her greatest dreams. As Giselle waits for Prince Edward to materialize and save her, she slowly comes to the realization that she has been waiting on the wrong prince all along.

Yes, Giselle had dreamed of *True Love's Kiss*, but that kiss wouldn't come from Edward. She had been waiting so long that she nearly settled for the first prince who arrived on the scene. Thankfully, the evil queen Nerissa intervened before it was too late and Giselle's "happily ever after" turned into an unhappy disaster. Fortunately for Giselle, this entire scenario ended up leading to an even happier ending than she had originally planned.

The unconventional twist of the story rests in the obvious mistake Giselle made in becoming so wrapped up in the wrong prince that she nearly missed the right one when he came along. Throughout the course of the movie, she repeatedly tells Robert (the man who takes her in from the streets and turns out to be her true prince) that Edward is coming for her. Day after day it is Edward, Edward, Edward. Only when a life-threatening disaster overtakes her does Giselle realize that Robert is her true "Prince Charming."

Ladies, we could learn a lot from Giselle because we, too, have had our eyes set on the wrong prince. When God first created the world, it was like a fairytale. Then the evil villain Satan came and pushed our world over the edge, transporting us to a place where there are no "happily ever afters"… or so we think. Because we're still clinging so tightly to the dream of our *prince*, we somehow fail to notice that our true *Prince* has already come. Why do we continue to miss this? Because our

Prince didn't come as we expected. He came from a faraway Kingdom that we didn't even realize was a kingdom at all. His majestic steed was a lowly donkey, and according to Isaiah 52, He wasn't all that attractive (*"He had no beauty or majesty to attract us to Him, nothing in His appearance that we should desire Him." v. 2*). In short, we missed our Prince because we were clinging to a dream.

According to our list of definitions, a third meaning for the word *wait* is *"to be hoping for something or on the lookout for something."* Here we are told to be "dreaming of a true love's kiss," but how, may I ask, are we supposed to be content with who we are and the way our life is if we are constantly searching for something more—for some romantic fantasy? How is one supposed to guard her heart when everything within her wants to give it away? Here's my advice: go ahead and give it away.

I heard that gasp, and yes, I can see the look of shock on your face. But before you slam the book closed and declare me crazy, perhaps I should expound upon my above statement. Go ahead and give your heart away… *to Jesus.* He is the only one who truly deserves it. I think one of the best pieces of advice I ever received was when my friend and mentor told me not to ask God to take my love away, but to ask for Him to redirect it. We are relational creatures because God made us that way. He gave us hearts that desire to love, and love we shall. But who and what receives our affection is up to us to decide.

Most single girls are tired of hearing others say that Jesus is a substitute for a husband, and I can relate to that. After all, the married women get to be the Bride of Christ too, so the whole "Jesus replacement" thing just isn't cutting it. But I'm even more tired of seeing that statement lived out the other way around when we turn our husbands, or boyfriends, or "significant others" into a substitute for a relationship with Jesus. Have you ever considered that maybe it's not so much that others are trying to cram God into your "guy-hole" as it is that you are trying to cram a guy into your "God-hole"?

> *Have you ever considered that maybe it's not so much that others are trying to cram God into your "guy-hole" as it is that you are trying to cram a guy into your "God-hole"?*

Just recently, I read a Christian dating book in which the author stated, "I'm tired of 'dating' Jesus... and I think the feeling is mutual." While I recognized the whole "Jesus is not a substitute for a man" argument, I couldn't help but cringe. I don't think Jesus gets tired of "dating" you. The Bible repeatedly tells us that God is a jealous God. Why would He ever tire of spending time with you? And while it's okay to want a "real" date every once in awhile, don't let it consume you. No man will ever be able to fill both your guy-hole and your God-hole. But God.... well, He's big enough to handle both of them. So go ahead and lose yourself in the magic and wonder of His love.

HE TOUCHED ME

I'll never forget the day I found my true Prince. I was sitting on the bed in a beach house, reading a book that my mom had picked up from the library when, suddenly, Jesus appeared. The God I had known all my life stepped down from His throne. He came to me from a land that was so far away, I thought I could never reach Him. I never believed I could touch Him—until He extended His hand, inviting me to dance with Him. No, I couldn't actually see Him in the physical sense, but I could see Him with my heart, and in that moment, it was all that mattered.

I tried to imagine Jesus as He is described in Isaiah—unattractive, unappealing—but His glory shone so brightly, and His eyes... Oh, those eyes! Those ever-changing, piercing, unfathomable eyes. They were, without a doubt, His most captivating feature. So much grace and compassion flowed forth from them. Throughout the years, I've seen many different expressions reflected in that deep gaze. I've seen the joy that flickers through them when I am dancing in His arms. I've seen them light up in laughter as we spin and twirl and I giggle with delight as I beg Him to spin me again and again. Sadly, I've also seen those same eyes wrestle with disappointment when I repeatedly pull away from Him and chase after the things He has begged me to avoid. And I've watched those eyes shine brightly with unconditional love and forgiveness when I come rushing back to His arms again.

I've often wondered what it would have been like to live during Biblical times. When I think of the women who followed Jesus throughout His ministry on earth, I cannot help but wonder about His eyes. About His touch. What would it have been like to stare the King of the universe straight in the face? And when Jesus reached out and touched the leper, what must that have been like? How does it feel to have the Shaper of the stars rest His hand on your shoulder? And then I realized that I *have* seen those eyes, and I have felt His touch. Even though He wasn't standing before me in the flesh, His touch was nonetheless real. Though no one who observed my dance could see, Jesus was there, and He was very real to me.

If you are reading this and thinking that you've never felt His presence in such a manner, let me assure you that you can feel it today. Invite Jesus to come, and expect Him to be there. But be prepared, because I can guarantee you that when He shows up, it will blow your mind. He may appear to you differently than He did to me. And that is to be expected. Since God knows every single detail about each and every one of us, He also knows your needs are different than mine. I'm a very intimate, physical, relational person; therefore, God needed to reveal Himself to me in a very intimate, physical, and relational way. The point is that you ask Him to come.

DON'T GO BREAKIN' HIS HEART

One of my co-workers once told me that you can reach a point in your relationship with Jesus where you will never be surprised. I looked at him kind of skeptically and remarked on how boring life would be without surprises. But he insisted it wasn't like that. The more I thought about it, the more I realized he was right. Sometimes, I feel this inner awareness that God is about to do something. Although I may not know exactly what it is that is coming, somehow I just know God is going to move in some way, shape or form. There is a sense of expectancy and anticipation as I wait for Him. Basically, I think the point my co-worker was trying to make is that you can know God like you know your best friend.

For example, my friend Josh and I have apparently spent way too much time together. I used to call him from my home phone, and even though two of my brothers were also friends with him, any time I would call, Josh would answer the phone, "Hey there, Miss Rebekah." He also seemed to always know what I wanted. If I was calling to ask a question, he would often answer that question before I even had a chance to ask. I would then hang up the phone, come out of my room, and ask my mom, "How does he do that?" Of course, I got pretty good at predicting him as well. If someone would make a comment, I would imagine exactly what Josh would reply, only to hear those words proceed from his mouth a moment later. Sometimes we even say the same thing at the same time, and because of this, we are constantly telling each other things like, "Get out of my brain."

I suppose one's relationship with God should look something like that. You need to know Jesus so well that you can hear His voice responding in different situations. You need to spend enough time in His presence that you won't be taken by surprise when He calls your name. In short, you need to share your heart with Him, and let Him share His heart with you.

I used to wonder why I should even bother to pray when God already knows exactly what I'm going to say. Well, in that case, I guess I could ask myself why I even bother talking to Josh. Maybe it's because I like being with him. Did you ever think that maybe God *likes* hearing from you? After all, the reason God created Adam was so He could have a relationship with him. He created Eve because Adam was lonely. But God never intended for Eve to take first place in Adam's life. I cannot help but wonder if God ever regrets His decision to create relationships between humans when He sees the way we chase after those relationships with the passion He intended for us to give to Him.

You didn't believe God was capable of regretting His decisions? What about the story of Noah and the ark, when He erased thousands of people from the face of the earth? Here is what we are told about the state of our world in those days: "The Lord observed the extent of the people's wickedness, and he saw that all their thoughts were consistently and totally evil. So the Lord was sorry he had ever made them. It broke his heart" (Gen. 6:5-6 NLT).

Did you catch that? You are capable of breaking God's heart, just as you are capable of breaking the heart of any man you may date. And just as you must be very careful with the heart of that young man, you must be even more careful with the heart of your Redeemer. God is a jealous God (Deut. 32:16). He won't be content to share you with another.

I think we tend to read the Bible and pick out the verses that appeal to us without considering the context of the verses around them. Take for example, Jeremiah 29:11: "'For I know the plans I have for you,' declares the Lord, 'plans to prosper you and not to harm you, plans to give you hope and a future.'" We pull this verse out—and plaster it on plaques and blankets and bookmarks—because we want this to be our story. We want God to take the tough places of our lives and make them something beautiful. What we fail to take into consideration is that this promise applied to a nation that would be held captive for seventy years. Do you want that to be your story? I also find the two verses following verse eleven to be extremely important. "Then you will call upon me and pray to me, and I will listen to you. You will seek me and find me *when you seek me with all your heart*" (Jer. 29:12-13, emphasis added).

All too often, we want to claim the promise of this scripture without expending any energy. God has great and glorious plans for you—which He will reveal *if you seek Him with all your heart.* Just as you chase after your dreams with every ounce of strength within you, how much more do you need to strive after God? It's time to take all of that effort you have exerted into finding a prince and redirect it toward your One True Prince.

> *It's time to take all of that effort you have exerted into finding a prince and redirect it toward your One True Prince.*

LORD OF THE DANCE

It was a big moment for me, the day I walked up those wooden steps that would lead me to the first formal dance I would ever attend. I felt like a princess. I wore a delicate gown that sparkled in the fading sunlight, and my hair cascaded in an array of curls down my back. When I entered the makeshift ballroom, I was overwhelmed by all the beautiful colors and styles that were so gracefully displayed by the other girls. As the time grew near for the dancing to begin, I grew more and more uncomfortable. I looked around at the roomful of strangers and began questioning why I had even come.

Reluctantly pushing my hesitations to the side, I attempted to enjoy the evening, regardless of how uncomfortable I felt dancing in the arms of unfamiliar young men. After a couple of dances, my salvation arrived. He walked through the open door, sending a wave of relief flooding over my anxious heart. Without a moment's pause, I made my way across the room and fell into place beside my friend Jessy—the only guy there with whom I felt completely comfortable.

"Hey," he smiled when I playfully punched his arm. Then he invited me to dance, and oh, what a dance it was! We tripped over one another's feet, laughing at our own clumsiness. Neither one of us had a clue what we were doing, but we were enjoying ourselves immensely as we tried to keep up with the footwork.

Somewhere amidst the partner changes, I ended up with a guy who really knew how to dance. I was quite literally "swept off my feet" the first time he spun me around, but I quickly caught onto his rhythm and we floated gracefully across the floor. For a moment, I was captivated by the thrill of this dance, but when the moment was over, I was reminded of the awkwardness of dancing with someone I hardly knew. I must confess that I was a little relieved when I found Jessy again.

When my mom arrived to pick me up, the dance was still going strong. She watched from the sidelines until I was free to go, and on the drive home, she shared her insight with me. "I could tell you were having fun," she said, "but you were never more you than when you were dancing with Jessy."

Well, duh. The thought floated to my mind before I could stop it. Of course I was more comfortable dancing with Jessy than anyone else. Of course that would be obvious to anyone observing. Then in that moment, my mind transported me back to the time of another dance. A dance that had occurred in the bedroom of a beach house. The real revelation hit me as God revealed to me a simple truth that has since transformed my life… Just as I was uncomfortable at the dance in the arms of all those others, I will always be uncomfortable dancing with the world. Security cannot be found in the arms of anyone save Jesus. His dance is flawless; His dance is divine; and the only time you will get your toes stepped on is when you try to go your own way. God intended for you and me to dance with Him, and people can see when we are not living according to that calling. It's true you know, you are never more "you" than when you dance in His arms, and you will never be wholly alive in anything but Him. He is the One who gives you purpose. More than that, He *is* your purpose.

The relationship God desires to have with us is as intimate as dancing face to face. Why else would He admonish the children of Israel with statements such as, "You have forsaken your first love" (Rev. 2:4), and "You have lived as a prostitute with many lovers— would you now return to me?" (Jer. 3:1). Jesus is the ultimate Prince of any fairytale, and He is inviting you to be a part of His divine love story. The Knight has set out on His next conquest, and that is to win and woo His beloved. You are His first love, but the question remains: *Is He yours?*

DRAGON-SLAYER

When I graduated high school, I received a letter from a precious ninety-year-old woman who had once given me piano lessons. She wrote about some of the many ways she had been blessed throughout the course of her life. It was one of those letters that you would expect to end with the words, "God has been so good," but imagine my shock when I got to the bottom of the letter to find the words, "Jesus has been so real."

I realized that Alberta had summed up ninety years in those five words, and in that moment, I decided that when I had lived ninety full years, those are the words that I would want to remember most clearly. *Jesus is real.* His love is real. His sacrifice is real. He is so overwhelmingly, wonderfully, powerfully, inexplicably, you-wouldn't-believe-it *real.*

I think we often fail to see how truly wonderful Jesus is. For the first fourteen years of my life, I didn't see it either. I knew in my heart that, yes, Jesus loves me (thanks to the popular song that is every church-attending child's first solo). And I knew that God gave His only Son to die in my place. But then He went back to heaven—which seemed so very, very far away. And in the course of day-to-day living, I too easily forgot the realness of my God.

God is awesome, and He is also omnipresent. Do you know what that means? It means He is every-where—at the same time. It means He isn't just sitting in heaven until the day He decides to return and vanquish Satan forever. It means He is with you *right now*. I guess I was wrong to say that Jesus suddenly appeared in the bedroom of that beach house. In truth, He was there all along, but I had only just taken notice. My question for you is: Have you taken notice of Him in your life? Or is He standing there, yet unseen, extending His hand in invitation for you to join Him in the dance of a lifetime?

Ephesians 5:25 contains that famous verse, "Husbands, love your wives, just as Christ loved the church and gave himself up for her." Marriage is really a picture of God's perfect relationship with us. And fairytales? Well, they are mere allegories of the true Prince who will one day come sweeping though the clouds on His gallant steed to carry the beautiful young maiden home to live with Him in heavenly bliss. The Prince of Peace stands before you at this moment in time, and He is more awesome and real than any of your imaginings. He is more real than any other man on the planet.

> *Don't allow your arms to stay so filled with the world's counterfeit dreams that you have no room for Him to come and sweep you into His dance.*

You are being sought after by the King of the universe, but are you too busy dreaming of your artificial Prince Charming to notice? Just like Giselle from *Enchanted*, you may be overlooking your true Prince because you are so caught up in another. Don't allow your arms to stay so filled with the world's counterfeit dreams that you have no room for Him to come and sweep you into His dance.

Wake up, Sleeping Beauty, or you will miss Him. Because you sleep, you cannot see that your Prince has fought His way through the thorns—a crown of thorns—and is steadily making His way to your side. Your dreams are so small, your vision too narrow. But when at last you open your eyes, you will find that your Prince is no mortal man, and the kiss that awakened you was the kiss of One who would give His life so that you might live. His love thunders from the cross, interwoven with the anguished cries of a sacrifice made on your behalf. Those are the cries of a Man in love. Your Prince is slaying the dragon, even if it may first appear that the dragon is slaying Him.

Ancient folklore tells of maidens being sacrificed to appease the dragon. But princess, this life is more than folklore, and you were the maiden chosen this time around. Your life was hanging in the balance, about to be offered as a sacrifice to the great dragon. Then Jesus intervened. In a heroic effort more fantastical than the wildest fiction, He stepped in and surrendered Himself in your place. But in this Fairytale, the One who gives His life so unselfishly cannot lose. And so He lives to be with you. Look no further, young maiden. Your Prince is here.

Chapter 4

The Things Only
God Knows

Waiting Defined:
To be Delayed or Ignored for Now

"I'll do my dreaming with my eyes
wide open, and I'll do my looking back
with my eyes closed."

-Tony Arata

As I mentioned in Chapter One, I spent three years of my life crushing on one particular guy. In my young mind, this was love. He was the man I was going to spend the rest of my life with. He was the prince from my fairytale. After years of dreaming, the day of the wedding finally came, but I wasn't the girl in the white dress staring adoringly into his eyes… and I'm glad. Maybe I didn't always feel that way, but I'm truly happy now.

I still remember the day he first introduced me to his new girlfriend. In that very moment, I knew she was different from any of the other girls he had dated for a time. What I didn't realize immediately was that my recognizing the difference was God's way of protecting me. Somehow I sensed that I would live to witness their wedding day. Thankfully, by the time the wedding actually rolled around, I was over him, but there was still that thought in my mind that I had wasted years dreaming. If only I could have reclaimed those wasted years. If only I could have refocused my worthless dreams. If only, if only, if only.

During the month leading up to the wedding, I spent a lot of time on my knees. My prayers started out as heartfelt cries of, "God, why? I really thought he was the one. I truly thought this was *my* happy ending. I don't understand." However, over time, those prayers slowly changed to the point that, when I sat in the sanctuary watching this guy pledge his heart to another woman, my prayer was, "Thank you, God, that I'm *not* the girl in the white dress."

What happened to change my hopes and dreams? I threw all the energy I had been devoting to this guy toward my Heavenly Father instead. I asked Him to take the broken pieces of my heart and make them like new. I prayed that He would give me His eyes to see light in a situation where, at the time, I saw nothing but darkness. And God was faithful to answer my cries. His Light seeped in with a promise: "I have something better for you, My child. My plans—My dreams—are so much bigger than yours."

I began to understand that God did have something so much bigger waiting just around the corner. Instead of only seeing how wonderful this guy was, I started to see how he didn't fit in with my hopes and dreams. Slowly, I realized that I couldn't have both my dreams and him, and if one had to go, it was most definitely going to be him. He had, of course, already made this decision for me, but I was pretty determined to let go of him with my own free will. On that day when God told me that His dreams were bigger than my own, I saw that my dreams were indeed too small, so I decided to spend the rest of my life becoming part of the bigger dream—God's dream for me. It was time to let God govern every part of my life. It was time to follow after the things I could not see, with my eyes wide open to pursue and trust the God who was offering to reveal them to me.

PUSHING THE ENVELOPE

Recently, the ladies in my office sent a co-worker and his wife on a weekend adventure. Our ringleader, who is extremely adventurous by nature, decided it just wasn't right that this couple never went out and did anything for themselves. Since they didn't have kids of their own to encourage them to do such things, we became their self-declared, honorary children for a weekend.

One afternoon at work, we presented this couple with a gift bag containing sixteen precious envelopes. We guaranteed them that each envelope had been approved by "Mr. Fun" and then explained that there was only one rule to this adventure: they could not fail to follow the exact instructions each envelope contained. The envelopes, of course, enclosed detailed instructions on where to go, but also insisted that the other envelopes could not be opened until specific times, or it would ruin the surprise.

Our co-worker was skeptical, to say the least. He didn't want the surprise. He wanted to know exactly where he was going. He wanted to be sure of what the weekend held. I'm told that when he opened the envelope explaining he was going out of state, he had quite a breakdown. "My worst nightmare is coming true," he exclaimed. "My life is being controlled by five, conniving, scheming women!" (His wife later told us that this was the "pretty" version of what actually happened.) That was Friday. When Tuesday rolled around and we were all back in the office, our friend was thanking us repeatedly. What caused this change of attitude? Well, by the time the last envelope was opened, he realized that while it was totally unexpected, the adventure was greater than he could have dreamed it to be.

I like to think God directs our lives much like we directed our co-workers' lives that weekend. He unfolds the adventure piece by piece—or envelope by envelope, if you will. It can be absolutely horrifying to not know where you are going, to not be able to see what is coming around the corner... Or it can be a beautiful adventure. If you asked my co-worker, he would tell you that the journey was much more enjoyable after he had gotten a little further into it and realized that we truly did have his best interest in mind. We had done our research, and every step he took led him to something he thoroughly enjoyed.

It's wise to remember that God knows you better than you know yourself. If the girls in my office could plan such an exciting adventure for a co-worker we don't know half as well as we know ourselves, how much greater is the adventure God has in store for you? It's like that promise God gives us in Jeremiah 29. He has plans to prosper us, if only we seek Him with our whole hearts. We must first listen for His voice, or we risk never knowing His plans for our lives.

My co-worker's whole weekend could have been ruined if he had opened the envelopes out of order or chosen not to follow one of the instructions we had given him. Every single envelope had a purpose;

each one was leading him to his final destination—the grand finale so to speak. He, of course, didn't realize this. The instructions never made sense to him until the very end when he looked back through the envelopes and said, "Now I get it!"

In similar fashion, I believe our lives are very much like that weekend adventure. One day when you look back over the course of your life and see where God has led you, you will be able to say, "Now I get it." Everything will begin to fall into place. Little by little, things will start making sense. Until then, you have to trust that the One who put the envelopes of your life together is only thinking of your best interests.

DELAY: A LETDOWN OR A LIFESAVER?

Most days, we tend to feel that the "envelope" containing our future husband has been waiting far too long. We relate all too well with the fourth definition of wait: *"To be delayed or ignored for now."* Let me try and help clear up a few things in your mind. For starters, God is *not* ignoring you. He knows the desires of your heart, and He also knows what you ultimately need. Now that you know you are never ignored, let's deal with how it feels to be *delayed* for a time. Delayed. That's not a fun word, is it? It tends to conjure up the same feelings as the word *wait*, and I guess that it would, considering that it's used in this definition. But before you assume the whole husband flight is canceled, I think there are two big things you should know about being delayed.

First off, let me assure you that being delayed is not always a bad thing. We immediately tend to associate delay with being late for something or inconvenienced because we've been held up or slowed down. Our irritation at these things most often stems from the impatient part of our nature, but did you know that delays have actually saved lives? According to one of those "forward me" emails that found its way to my inbox, there were several people who should have been in the World Trade Center when 9/11 happened. The reasons these people were spared the tragedy is because they were delayed by traffic, had alarm clocks that didn't go off, missed the bus, or had to change the clothes they spilled food on... There was even one report of a man who stopped at a convenience store to buy a bandage for his blister. These were all things that probably irritated these people at the time. After all, they were running late for work because of all these inconveniences. Funny how an inconvenience turns into a blessing when it comes to saving lives.

Have you ever considered that the delay in the arrival of your husband could be a blessing? In fact, it could be saving your life. You may think that is a little drastic to say, but I truly believe that God could be saving you from a lifetime of heartache by delaying your future husband for the time being.

> *Have you ever considered that the delay in the arrival of your husband could be a blessing?*

Perhaps one or both of you isn't ready. In fact, if God is holding off for awhile, you're probably safe to assume this is true. Oh, I know, we think we're ready, but if God were to give us everything we think we want today, we would be in for a rude awakening. We are still very much like that young child who *thinks* she is big enough to cross the road by herself, *thinks* she is old enough to navigate the big woods all by herself, *thinks* she is old enough to watch scary movies with her big siblings. (Don't you just remember the nightmares?)

When I look at my thirteen-year-old sister, all I can see is how young she is. But I remember being thirteen, and I didn't feel I was that young. I *thought* I was practically an adult. I *thought* I was so mature, so grown-up, so ready to tackle the world. Now when I look at all those things I thought when I was thirteen, I can't help but laugh. I wasn't ready to take on the world. Sometimes I feel like I'm still not ready. I often wish I could go back and redo those days. I wish I could live them with the childish innocence I was so anxious to forfeit. And I'll bet that when the day comes that you finally marry your prince, you will look back at all those years you spent leading up to that special moment. I hope you don't have any regrets. I hope you can look back and cherish the life that you lived and the memories you made when you had the freedom to live alone with God. I hope you see that you were not yet ready to have the responsibilities of being a wife thrust upon you. And I really, really hope that you are thankful for the years you remained single.

DELAY ≠ DENIAL

The second thing I want you to realize is something that was told to me many years ago. *Delay does not mean denial.* Sometimes we feel as if the fact that we are not yet married means we never will be. We are doomed to be single forever—an old maid. Now there's a phrase that strikes terror into the heart of many a single girl. Don't worry. While that may be the life to which God has called some people, you will most likely marry someday. The best thing to do in the meantime is to simply trust that God has everything—marriage plans and all—in His hands and let Him take care of it.

So often we buy into the lie that we must seek our prince. We wonder how we will ever find him if we don't search for him. Might I mention that if God is withholding your prince for a time, you're not going to find him no matter how hard you try. Your hopes are futile. Your search is in vain. Calm down. This is not your worst nightmare. After all, your life is not in the hands of "five, conniving, scheming women," but in the hands of a loving, heavenly Father. You can rest assured that God is only thinking of what is best for you, and His delay does not always mean His denial. Stop fretting that you'll never find a prince. I'm pretty sure you wouldn't want to marry whatever prince you might manage to discover on your own anyway. It's better to be content to let God find your prince for you, or you may end up finding yourself marrying a mistake. Or a toad, complete with nasty warts.

Perhaps we all need to be given a fresh perspective on "the waiting process." So listen up. You are not being delayed; you are being given a chance to live without obligations. You are not being denied a Prince Charming, but granted a season of life and adventure, so stop looking at the glass as if it is half empty. I find it ironic that we spend our single years wishing to be married when many older, married woman will tell you that "these are the best years of your life." Perhaps those words are meant to have a subtle challenge tagged on the end: "These are the best years of your life… *don't waste them*." I'm pretty much convinced that, as long as you intentionally live every moment of your life to the fullest, every year can be "the best years of your life."

THE MASTER OF DISGUISE

Like my parking garage dilemma from Chapter One, when we focus our attention on one single thing, we tend to miss all the other beautiful things that surround us. Being single does not equal being miserable or even lonely. In the absence of a spouse, Jesus becomes our lover. Perhaps the reason we are not born married is so God can firmly establish our love relationship with Him before our affections are divided between Him and another.

"Yet I hold this against you; You have forsaken your first love." I find that these words found in Revelation 2:4 have struck a chord in my heart on more than one occasion. We are so disconnected with the spiritual realm that we feel we need to be loved by someone we can see and touch. And so we stray from God's love in search of another, never realizing what we are missing by moving away from Him.

In the original story of Beauty and the Beast (as in, not the Disney one), Beauty is held captive by a hideous beast. Every night, she dreams of a handsome prince who begs her not to leave him until she has delivered him from his cruel fate. He warns her not to trust her eyes, but to find him no matter how he may be disguised. We, of course, know this was the beast who was indeed a prince under a spell, but Beauty is not fortunate enough to be privy to that vital piece of information. Every evening, the beast would ask Beauty to marry him, and every evening, she would refuse his proposal, thinking only of the prince from her dream—whom she believed must be held captive somewhere in the castle. The entire time, the man of her dreams was before her, yet she never realized that the prince and the beast were one and the same. Why? Her dreams revealed a prince in the way she always imagined a prince should look, but reality cast her prince in quite a "beastly" light.

> Whether we see Him or not, God is there in our everyday lives; we simply need to learn how to recognize Him.

I believe that God appears to us in a similar manner. While He may not come in the form of a hideous beast, He nonetheless looks different than we would have expected, and therefore, we do not see Him for who He is. But whether we see Him or not, God is there in our everyday lives; we simply need to learn how to recognize Him. He appears in butterflies fluttering on summer breezes, shooting stars lighting up the night sky, baby smiles and children's laughter, rainbows and flowers, oceans and thunderstorms, hugs and encouraging notes from a friend. He appears anywhere and everywhere if only you have the eyes to see Him—even when He is and is not as you would imagine Him to be.

Jesus once appeared to me in a way that was so real and intimate that I still bear the imprint of His touch today. And while I have memories of butterflies fluttering over ocean waves and rainbows lighting up the skies of my heart, this one moment in time is a moment I will cherish for the rest of my life. I still remember it all so clearly. I had been going through a really hard time, and as I sat before God that particular morning, completely broken, I prayed, "God, I wish You had physical arms, because I really need to be held right now." I must have been hurting so much that I forgot how big my God was because, even as I prayed, I wasn't truly expecting Him to wrap His arms around me.

I spent the rest of the day merely going through the motions before heading off to a youth meeting that night. I donned my best "plastic smile" and made it through the evening without anyone guessing that something was eating away at my insides. But as I said my final goodbyes, I turned around to find my friend Jared standing there with his arms outstretched. Now, Jared has hugged me before on several occasions, but perhaps because I needed to be held so badly, I nearly cried as I melted into His embrace. As I leaned my head against his chest, everything else melted away—my heartache, my situation, my surroundings—because in that moment it wasn't Jared who held me, but Jesus.

Through the arms of a friend, Jesus pulled me close and touched my heart. How long we stood there like that, I don't know. It was probably less than a minute, but it felt like an eternity that I rested in what I perceived to be God's everlasting arms. Even after the embrace was broken, the feeling of those arms remained tightly wrapped around my heart, and I knew that I was going to be okay. Even though my circumstances hadn't changed, even though there was still no end in sight to the pain, God had wiped away my tears, assuring me that He was taking care of everything. He had given me eyes to see Him in the embrace of a friend.

What does this have to do with being delayed, you wonder? When I looked for Bible verses containing the word *delayed*, I came to rest on two particular scriptures. The first verse I discovered was Isaiah 46:13 which says: "I am bringing my righteousness near, it is not far away; and my salvation will not be *delayed*. I will grant salvation to Zion, my splendor to Israel." The second verse was Ezekiel 12:23 which reads: "Therefore say to them, 'This is what the Sovereign Lord says: None of my words will be *delayed* any longer; whatever I say will be fulfilled, declares the Sovereign Lord" (emphasis added).

According to these verses, there are two things that will not be delayed, God's Salvation and God's

Word. Perhaps you are wondering why God has not yet "saved" you from singleness. Again, I don't believe singleness is a fate from which one needs to be saved, but rather, a gift to cherish. Regardless, more often than not, we fail to see God's salvation in light of how it truly is. We read these verses that state God's words and salvation will not be delayed, but we contort them into a promise that our deliverance is just around the corner. We would do well to remember that, just as God does not appear in the form that we would often expect, His salvation may come differently than we imagined, as well. Perhaps God has already arrived in answer to your prayers, but you simply failed to recognize Him through His disguise. After all, many people who had been waiting for the Messiah did not think Jesus could possibly be God's Chosen One because *He was nothing like they expected.*

> Perhaps God has already arrived in answer to your prayers, but you simply failed to recognize Him through His disguise.

Throughout the course of the struggle that had sent me falling into Jesus' (er, Jared's) arms, I underlined several verses in my Bible pertaining to God's deliverance. I pondered verses such as, "In my anguish I cried to the Lord, and he answered by setting me free" (Psalm 118:5) and "Then they cried out to the Lord in their trouble and he delivered them from their distress" (Psalm 107:6). I thought these were God's promises to fix the part of my life that was rapidly collapsing around me. But notice that God promises to deliver us from our distress, not the *situation* causing our distress. When I finally came to realize this, I could see that God was not delaying His salvation; I was simply refusing to accept it because it did not come in the form in which I expected it. I want you to realize that this is extremely important. Until I discovered what kind of freedom God was promising me in Psalm 118:5, I could not truly be set free.

YOUR DELIGHT IS MY DESIRE

I believe that, in order to be set free from the sting of loneliness that comes with desiring a husband, we must fully surrender our desires to Jesus. We must place our longings into His capable hands and trust that He will bring those desires back to us in due time. A verse many of us cling to with utmost fervency is Psalm 37:4 which states: "Delight yourself in the Lord and he will give you the desires of your heart." We pray this verse along with our prayers that plead, "God, I want a husband more than I've ever wanted anything in the world. Isn't this Your promise to bring him to me? Then where is he, God?"

I want to point out two things. Notice this verse never specifies *when* God is going to give you said desires, but more importantly, I want you to rewind to the first half of that verse—the one we so conveniently skip over without truly seeing. "Delight yourself in the

Lord." God will give you the desires of your heart *if* you delight yourself in Him. But I must warn you that *if* you delight yourself in Him, your desires have a tendency to change. You may start to see through His eyes. You may start to see something… better.

When you turn your eyes from your fantasies long enough to start pursuing something with your life, when you press on toward the goal God has purposed for you, and when you choose to make Him your First Love, you are delighting yourself in Him. And because He delights over you in return, you may begin to see the simple things He does just because He loves you. Because you are enraptured in Him, you will notice the butterflies and rainbows, sand dollars and birdsongs. These will become His love notes to you, the gentle reminders of a love that has come to set your heart free.

I know from experience that, after awhile, you will fail to notice that your earthly prince has been delayed for a time because your desires will have changed. Just as if you are in love, your desire will be for Jesus as His desire is for you. Your dream of being loved and cherished by a husband will remain, but it will be pushed aside for another day—for the proper time.

Is this scenario sounding impossible? Does it seem too perfect and unobtainable? I will confess that it's not easy to let everything go and leave it go. Sometimes I find that I'm not as close to God as I'd like to be. Other times I find that my dreams of princes and enchanted castles rise to the surface once more, and I wonder when my earthly prince will come. I wonder when God will release me to marry a man and raise a family. It is at times like these that I have to remind myself that I already have the love of a heavenly Prince, and I am a part of His family.

If you are dreaming of Prince Charming and feeling as if you are held captive by this beast called "Single-ness," let me just say, "Ah, Beauty, you are not so unfortunate as you suppose!" For it is in this so-called beast named Singleness that you will draw closer to the greatest Prince of all time. When you embrace single-ness, as Beauty did the beast, you may find that your true Prince was waiting for the moment you would free Him to love you as He desires. So go ahead and live the adventure. Enjoy every moment of your life. Embrace singleness for what it truly is, and do not be dismayed by the delay. Remember that *delay* does not necessarily mean *denial* nor is it always to be consid-ered a bad thing. In fact, you may find it is exactly as the sweet, older women say. These years *could* be the best years of your life… if only you will let them.

Chapter 5

Be Prepared...
To Be Used For
God's Glory

Waiting Defined:
Be Ready or Available for
Someone to Take or Use

*"Dream as if you'll live forever... live
as if you'll die today."*

-James Dean

So by this time, you know yourself intimately, are chasing your dreams without slowing down for anyone or anything, are so madly in love with Jesus that nothing else matters, and are perfectly content with who you are. Okay, so that may be a bit of a stretch, but I hope you are well on your way to embracing singleness. No matter how far you feel you have traveled on this journey, this is my question and challenge: Can we tell? Is it obvious to the world that you are not content to live a mediocre life? Can people see that you are not willing to simply settle for the norm? Does your life bear witness to the fact that you are pursuing much more than the average fairytale?

Our fifth definition of the word *wait* is: *"Be ready or available for someone to take or use."* Now, I'm not so fond of the thought of being used, but I do want to challenge you to be ready—ready to let the world know that you are someone who is completely sold out to Jesus.

When I was in high school, my youth group spent a week doing missions work in Atlanta, Georgia. I spent most of my free time hanging out with one of my guy friends, and the two of us apparently gave several people the impression that we were related. On one of our last nights in Atlanta, a girl from one of the other youth groups asked us if we were siblings. "You're the third person who has asked that this week," I cried, exasperated. "Do we really look that much alike?"

"It's not that you look alike," she shrugged. "You just seem really close."

My friend Jessy was the first to respond, and I couldn't help but smile at his assessment of our relationship. "I've always kind of seen her as a big sister/the same age."

I couldn't have said it better myself. This was honestly the way we viewed each other, and it was so clearly displayed through our actions that people mistook us to be biological siblings. I was myself around Jessy, just as Mom had noted when she watched the two of us dancing together that one night. Only this time it was complete strangers who were identifying him as my brother. Think about that for a moment: Complete strangers form opinions of you by the way you act. I hope that you are accused of loving Jesus.

I challenge you to fall so in love with Jesus that people will immediately identify you as His beloved. Give them the impression that you are related to the God of the universe, because, in a very real sense, you are. Ephesians 1:4-6 tells us, "For he [God] chose us in him before the creation of the world to be holy and blameless in his sight. In love he predestined us to be adopted as his sons through Jesus Christ, in accordance with his pleasure and will—to the praise of his glorious grace, which he has freely given us in the One he loves."

Did you hear that? You've been adopted by God

Himself. He chose you. Out of the billions of people on earth, He chose *you* to be His daughter. He invited *you* to be His beloved. You are His child, and according to Romans 8:39, "neither height nor depth, nor anything else in all creation, will be able to separate us from the love of God that is in Christ Jesus our Lord." Do you live like you believe that? Just as people saw me as Jessy's sister, let them see you as God's daughter.

It's generally easy to identify a person's family members. Though some families bear little physical resemblance, there is often a phrase or voice or mannerism that gives them away. At my graduation party, a friend of mine was sitting beside her dad when he pointed out my dad's two brothers to her. "You know them?" my friend asked in surprise.

"No," her father shrugged. "I can just tell." Far more than any physical resemblances, it was my uncles' voices and mannerisms that gave them away as my dad's brothers. They walked like Snyders, talked like Snyders, and carried themselves just like my dad. In the same manner, the way you walk, talk and act will show the world the depth of your relationship with Jesus. So let your love for God be evident. Allow your heart to become so caught up in Him that you have no need for anyone else. Know who you are, and be content with the person He has created you to be. Be satisfied with the place God has called you to— here and now. It's great to have hopes and dreams for the future, but don't let those dreams inhibit you from living in the present.

BE PREPARED... TO LIVE LIKE YOU'RE DYING

We sometimes tend to trudge through our single years as if we are waiting for the day life will begin—as if the day some man comes to sweep us off our feet will be the day we truly start living. I hate to break it to you, sister, but if you aren't living now, I highly doubt you will be living then. God is the Giver and Sustainer of life; the man you will one day marry is not. Any married person will tell you that their spouse does not "complete" them as you might expect a husband to complete you. God is the only One who can fill that void in your life. Our entire lives are leading up to the "happily ever after" with Him.

One of the missionaries supported by the organization I work with signs his email correspondences with the words "Live to Die." Perhaps the fact that his line of work is so dangerous causes him to be more aware of the fact that every moment of our lives is preparation for eternity spent with God. These years on earth are so few when compared to the life we will lead in heaven. We have to make every moment count. In essence, we must live like we are dying.

I'm sure you have heard that common question, "If you knew you had only one year left to live, what would you do?" Stop for a moment. Think about that question. I mean, really think about it. Form the answer in your mind. Do you have it yet? Don't read on until you do.

All right. What is keeping you from doing that thing? Why won't you pursue it? Why do you have to be dying in order to do that thing you've always wanted to do while you yet live? So many people will tell you that they are afraid of dying, but I'm inclined to believe that more of us are afraid to truly live—to step out and do what is in our hearts to do. At least, that's the impression I get from watching people walk through the same routine day in and day out.

I'm convinced that no life is worth living if it is not lived for God's glory. We must be prepared to follow God whenever and wherever He calls us to go. To be willing to step out into the unknown. To risk being ready for Him to pull us into the adventure of a lifetime. And believe me, He will… if you will only ask Him.

BE PREPARED… TO MAKE THE MOST OF THE MESSES

A pastor friend of mine once shared with his congregation that "Jesus just messes things up." He didn't say it like it was a bad thing, although he implied that he often finds it frustrating. He just stated that phrase like it was a fact—a fact that intrigued him. If you've been a Christian for any length of time, you'll most likely know what he was talking about. It's those moments when you think you have your life all planned out, then something comes up and you have to rework your plans. It's those times when you think you finally have your life under control, then something totally unexpected happens and you realize you're no longer in the driver's seat. There are really only two options when this happens. Either freak out, or enjoy the ride. Be assured that if you truly invite Jesus to rule your life, then you can also be assured that He will most likely "mess things up" from time to time.

I used to have my story all mapped out, complete with my own version of "happily ever after" and conspicuously free of "messes." Yes, I used to think I knew exactly what it was that I wanted in life. Then God came along, took my infinitely small, pre-conceived expectations, and turned them upside-down. While it may have been upsetting at the time, now I can say that I am honestly glad He did it. I'm thankful that I get to walk through life continually amazed by the things God is slowly unveiling in my story—one chapter at a time.

I'm learning to accept that life is much more exciting when I'm not the one controlling it. Seeing that I'm not nearly as creative as the Master Storyteller, I have a tendency to let every day pass just like the day before. After a while, I can find myself getting bored. One time, I got so tired of the mundane routine I had fallen into that I actually *asked* God to mess things up a little. I confess that I knew what a dangerous prayer that was, but I truly wanted Him to shake things up a bit. I was ready for a change of scenery.

When I was a little girl, I used to like to walk in the footprints my daddy left on the beach. As a matter of fact, I still do—it's a part of that childish wonder I try to hold onto. Determinedly, I would jump from one footprint to another, delighting in following the path my father had left for me. But I had to move quickly, before the waves came and removed any sign that my dad had been there only moments before. Often, the continuing waves made his footprints difficult to see, and sometimes even erased them completely.

Just as I had to be prepared to move quickly in order to place my feet in Daddy's footprints, so you must follow closely in the path God is creating for you, or you may miss it entirely. You need to be ready to move as soon as God starts moving, or you will find yourself already off-course. It's difficult to catch up once you miss a step, and sometimes, it is almost tempting to give up and stop following altogether because you feel you will never find

> *Although it's difficult to rediscover God's path, it's not completely impossible, and the joy of the journey is worth the effort involved in continuing the chase.*

the footprint before it is washed away by the wave. Although it's difficult to rediscover God's path, it's not completely impossible, and the joy of the journey is worth the effort involved in continuing the chase.

BE PREPARED... FOR CHANGE. IT'S A VITAL PART OF EVERY STORY.

Your typical storybook heroine is one who faces conflict, and conquers. The entire story hinges on the fact that the world is shifting around this one character; something is happening that will change her life forever. Without conflict, there is no story to tell. Still, most of us remain creatures of habit and cringe at the very thought of that dreaded word—*change*.

My office hosts a Bible Study every Thursday morning. One week, after everyone had settled into their chairs, the leader asked them to get up and exchange seats. It was interesting to note the reactions. Some people got really uncomfortable. Others even refused to move. The whole point of this exercise was to illustrate the fact that people are uncomfortable with change—even a change as simple as switching seats. Let's face it, most of us don't like to step outside of our comfort zones. We want to know what is coming just around the bend; we want to be certain of where our lives are going. Change is uncertain. It often makes us feel uncomfortable, sometimes uninformed, and almost always unprepared. But as I was reminded during this week's Bible Study, change is also something for which we must plan because, like the heroine in our favorite novel, change is a vital part of our story.

A friend of mine is in a time of transition right now. She will soon be moving halfway across the country in order to fulfill the calling God has placed on her life. It's a time of big changes for her. When we talked about her moving, she didn't sound too happy about it.

She didn't want to leave the life with which she was so familiar and that she so enjoyed. She explained to me that she had told God, "I am only moving because You want me to move. You know I wouldn't choose this on my own. So if You really want me to go, You will have to put joy in my heart."

I couldn't help but smile at her honesty. Sometimes, I just need to hear that I am not the only one who struggles with the calling God has given me. I find it refreshing to hear other people—especially people I love and respect as much as I do this friend—say that they have often had these kinds of conversations with God as well. To hear my friend ask God to place joy in her heart for this change made me realize that I need to ask God to do the same thing for me in my life. When change comes your way, it's okay to ask God for the joy to embrace it.

> *When change comes your way, it's okay to ask God for the joy to embrace it.*

Change is not easy, but it *is* necessary. Jesus came to earth to change the old laws. Wait, scratch that. He came to *fulfill* the law which would, in turn, cause the entire Jewish legal system to change permanently. A lot of people rejected Jesus because they weren't ready to change. Just look at the rich, young ruler in Matthew 19. He wasn't prepared to give up everything he had and follow Jesus, even though he had basically confessed his life was nothing without God.

I don't know about you, but I don't want to turn out like the rich, young ruler. I don't want to be so caught up in earthly things that I miss that which is eternal. Instead, I want to be like the disciples whom Jesus called, challenging them to lay down their nets and follow Him. According to Mark 1:18, "At once they left their nets and followed him." Those guys were prepared. They were ready to drop everything and pursue the one thing that truly mattered. That one thing was Jesus, and He is still the only thing really worth chasing after today.

In order to live the fairytale life we all dream of, we must be willing to embrace change. We must release all of our hesitations and allow God to bring what He will as we prepare ourselves to be ready for Him to call us out and change everything. I feel I have to warn you that the change may not be something that you will necessarily like, at least not initially. Cinderella was surely not overjoyed at the death of either of her parents, and Beauty certainly was not thrilled to be held captive by a beast. But these things were vital to the story that was being told through their lives. And just like Beauty and Cinderella, we must be prepared for a few hard changes while still trusting that God has a beautiful ending in store for us.

BE PREPARED… TO FOLLOW HIS VOICE AND RAISE YOUR OWN

Christianity is not appealing to the world. Do you know why? Because Christians are not living as

God commanded them to live. They are not allowing themselves to be transformed by God's light. There are many people who have claimed Jesus as their Savior, but refuse to be completely cut off from the darkness of the world. We are still clinging to the way things were before we gave God all that we are. Or have we really given Him *all* that we are? Is there something you are withholding from the One who gave you everything? Do you truly believe what you claim to believe? If God is Someone worth believing in, I think He is worth believing in with everything I have within me. I think He is worth giving everything I've got.

Have you ever played the game, "Marco Polo?" It's basically just like tag except it's played in water and the person who is "It" must close his eyes while saying the word, "Marco." Everyone else in the pool has to answer, "Polo." The point of the game is for "It" to tag someone else just by following the sound of their voices, while everyone else keeps their eyes open and tries to avoid the person who is "It." I used to play this game with my cousins. One day, my cousin Jarod was trying to see how close he could get to the person who was "It" without actually getting caught. As you can probably imagine, Jarod was "It" nearly half of the game. After playing for awhile, Jarod realized that he had tagged everyone in the pool at least once. Everyone, that is, except me. This presented a challenge for him, and he decided he was not going to give up until he had caught me. But I was not going to go down without a fight. The game started up again with Jarod accidentally grabbing the wrong person, forcing my cousins to slowly leave the pool one by one. Eventually, the only people left in the pool to tag were my younger brother Josiah and me.

I figured Jarod would be able to catch me easily at that point. That is, until Josiah began to mimic my voice. After having spent thirteen years of his life with me, he was pretty good at imitating me. I watched Jarod circle the pool getting closer and closer to Josiah. Suddenly, Jarod lunged out and grasped Josiah's arm. He didn't even have to open his eyes to realize his mistake. "You're not Rebekah, are you?" he asked.

My little sister, apparently feeling sympathy for Jarod who was listening to Josiah lord his failure over him, decided to give Jarod a hand. Instead of having to cry "Marco" and listen for my answering "Polo," all Jarod had to do was listen to Lydia telling him which direction to go. Using this strategy (what I like to call "cheating"), he was able to catch me.

I learned several important lessons that day that I would like to share with you right now. For starters, it is imperative that you learn to know God's voice as well as Josiah knew mine. Because of how much time Josiah had spent listening to my voice, he could convince Jarod—who should have known my voice— into thinking he was actually me. In similar fashion, only when you learn to imitate God's voice can you accurately portray Him to the world.

Secondly, you must be willing to pursue God with as much determination as Jarod put into pursuing me. He would not be content to leave that pool until he was able to say he had caught me. Might I add, Jarod got so excited when he finally did catch me that I nearly drowned when he hoisted my ankle up in the air in victory. We should approach our relationship with God in this same manner. Don't leave this life without being able to say that you have reached Him, and in the process, get excited over your victories.

Lastly, we must follow God's directions as intently as Jarod followed my sister's instructions. If Jarod had not gone where Lydia told him to go, I might still be in that pool waiting on him today. Okay, so maybe that's a bit of an exaggeration since I was on the verge of just letting him catch me as it was. But just as Jarod needed someone giving him directions in order to catch me, you need God to give you directions explaining where to place your next step along this pathway of life. Isaiah 30:21 says, "Whether you turn to the right or to the left, your ears will hear a voice behind you, saying, 'This is the way; walk in it.'" You need to be prepared to follow that Voice wherever it may call you.

We Christians tend to become so caught up in the things of the world that it is often difficult to tell the difference between sinners and saints. Our actions reflect the world's "voice" just as surely as Josiah's voice imitated mine. Although we are called to be in the world, we are definitely not called to be *of* it. Jesus clearly states this when He prays for His disciples in John 17. Notice how He compares His disciples to Himself. "I have given them your word and the world has hated them, for they are not of the world any more than I am of the world. My prayer is not that you take them out of the world but that you protect them from the evil one. They are not of the world, even as I am not of it. Sanctify them by the truth; your word is truth. As you sent me into the world, I have sent them into the world" (John 17:14-18).

We have a purpose on this earth. God has not yet taken us *out* of the world, but rather, sent us *into* the world with the challenge to live as Jesus lived. You must be prepared to allow God to sanctify you by the truth of His Word and be ready to be transformed by His saving grace. Only after His light has penetrated the darkest parts of your soul will you truly be ready to live. And only in living freely and shining purely will your reflection of God be of meaning or value to others.

BE PREPARED... TO DANCE LIKE A FOOL WITH A SPARKLER.

Last Fourth of July, I was sitting in my front yard watching fireworks when a friend of mine lit a sparkler, handed it to me, and encouraged me to "do a sparkler dance." I wasn't quite sure what a "sparkler dance" was, but I got up and twirled about the darkened yard to the music of laughter. For a brief instant, all I could think was, "I can't believe I'm doing this. *Why* am I doing this?" It didn't take me long to come up with the answer. I was doing this crazy dance because I was certain of the approval in the eyes of those around me. I knew they wouldn't judge me for the way I conducted myself, so I was free to goof off and simply be "me" in their presence. I never would have done such a thing if I was not confident of their love, but because I was certain of my standing in their eyes, I danced like a fool with a sparkler.

It's exhilarating to live in that kind of freedom. There is no greater joy than to know you are accepted as you are—the good, the bad, and the silly. The King of the universe has accepted you and invites you to dance in His light. Matthew 5:16 says, "In the same way, let your light shine before men, that they may see your good deeds and praise your father in heaven." It's time to let your light shine. It's time to let the truth you have learned saturate your entire being and affect the way you live. It's time to show the world that you were made for so much more than the life for which others are settling.

Live intentionally. You have a purpose; you have a calling. You are being prepared to be someone much greater than you could possibly imagine. And you know what? God wants that for you. John 10:10 tells us that Jesus came so that we could have life to the full. That means He intended for you to truly live, not just meander through a dull existence. Jesus is going to rock your world. Be

> *God will never take advantage of you. He will never break your heart and leave you to pick up the pieces.*

ready for—and expectant of—the moment He comes and gets the party started.

If one must be ready or available for someone to take or use, I can't think of anyone better to entrust my life to than the One who spoke me into being. Hear this clearly, my friend: God will never take advantage of you. He will never break your heart and leave you to pick up the pieces. So be prepared for a love that exceeds your dreams. Brace yourself for the adventure of a lifetime.

> *Be ready or available...*
>
> *to follow His Voice wherever it may lead you.*
>
> *Be ready or available...*
>
> *to show someone how God's love has completely transformed your life.*
>
> *Be ready or available...*
>
> *to stand up for your convictions and let your light shine brightly for all of the world to see.*
>
> *Be ready or available...*
>
> *to be taken and used for God's glory.*

Be prepared for the moment when God hands you His Light and asks you to let it shine in the darkness. Wave it high; wave it proudly; and dance like a woman who is certain of her calling. Dance as one who is completely captivated by God's love. Dance as one who is secure and wholly accepted. Dance like a fool with a sparkler... for all the world to see.

Chapter 6

Single By Choice

Waiting Defined:
Delay Something

"When we single women stop asking, 'Why am
I alone?' and start asking, 'Why am I here?' our
whole world will change – for the good."

-Michelle McKinney Hammond

For those of you who had to do a double-take at the title of this chapter, allow me to jump right into definition number six: *"Delay something."* This is quite different from being delayed. *Being delayed* is something that happens to you, while *delaying something* is a thing you choose to do of your own free will. I can hear some of you gasping already at the very idea of *choosing* singleness. After all, isn't it the dream of every woman to someday be married?

Unfortunately, our culture has force-fed us the lie that if you don't have a desire for a romantic relationship, there is something wrong with you. Don't misunderstand me, I fully expect most of you to have a desire to marry just as I do, and I'm not asking you to give up your dream of being a wife someday; I'm merely suggesting that you stop dreaming about being married *this* day. You don't have to choose singleness forever (unless, of course, God has called you to a life of celibacy, in which case I highly recommend you follow through with that calling), but I do encourage you to embrace singleness for a season.

If you attended Sunday School for any length of time, you are probably familiar with the Bible story of Esther. She was the young Jewish maiden whose beauty captured the heart of a king, and whose role as his chosen queen then saved an entire race of people from annihilation. But if you've never heard the story, or if your mind is a little fuzzy on the details, I'd encourage you to read her history in the book of Esther. If you don't read it, you may miss the importance of what I'm about to say. So just set this book down and come back when you've finished.

It would take another entire book to explore all the facets of Esther's story but I am going to zero in on one single verse that I feel is necessary to know about Esther. Esther 2:12 says, "Before a girl's turn came to go in to King Xerxes, she had to complete twelve months of beauty treatments prescribed for the women, six months with oil of myrrh and six with perfumes and cosmetics."

Esther had to spend an entire year in preparation before she would be summoned to meet the King. She would not be ready to wear the crown until she had gone though all the necessary treatments. Just as Esther was not prepared to be a queen, you and I are not yet ready to be wives. God has not finished preparing us. We have not yet completed the task He intended for us to accomplish during our single years.

Although we are told that Esther was given twelve months of preparation, we are never told what she did—aside from those mandatory beauty treatments. There is no verse that says, "And during the course of those twelve months, Esther drew ever closer to God and grew more attentive to His voice." There's not even a verse that says, "And every day, for twelve months, she prayed that she would be God's choice as the king's bride." Nothing. Nada. Zilch.

Perhaps God chose not to share this information with us because He didn't feel it was necessary for us to know what Esther did with her year of preparation. Perhaps He left this question to our imaginations because the only thing that is truly relevant to our lives today is what we choose to do with *our* time of preparation. Here and now.

I want to ask you a very pointed question. Why are you single? If you answered, "Well, I'm single because I can't seem to get a date," then I hope your perspective will change shortly, because there is a real joy found in truly *choosing* singleness.

CONTENT TO BE ME, SINGLE THOUGH I MAY BE

When I was growing up, my parents had a rule about dating. None of us kids were allowed to date until we turned sixteen. Over the period of time that I was outside the "dating circle," I observed the relationships of my friends around me. And by the time I turned sixteen, I had absolutely no desire to date anybody. Why? I watched too many girls lose their identities when they started dating a guy. One minute they were my childhood friends, but after a few weeks, I hardly recognized them anymore.

Remember the movie *Runaway Bride*? Julia Roberts' character molded herself into becoming whoever her newest boyfriend wanted her to be because she didn't know who she truly was. I think the reason she consistently ran before she reached the altar was because, even though she wasn't sure exactly who she was, she had learned enough to know who she *wasn't* and she didn't want to live the rest of her life as that girl.

Sadly, this story isn't just a movie plot. There are many girls in real life who are having the same struggle as the fictional Maggie Carpenter. In fact, a friend of mine once confessed to having a similar problem. She would claim to like a guy's favorite sports team, favorite music, favorite color, etc. After growing tired of changing her views to match those of the man she was currently dating, she went to an online dating site just to fill out the information that is required to set up a dating profile. She did this because she wanted to have to think about her likes and dislikes. She needed to be able to say, "This is who I am, and I am not changing that for anyone or anything." That is why I recommended writing your list in Chapter One. It's imperative that you get to know yourself, or you may "find" yourself losing yourself in the next guy who comes along. You need to learn to be content with who you are as a single woman—not as the girl-friend of some cute guy.

Contentment is a word that makes most of us flinch—probably because we know we aren't content even though we should be. Exactly what is contentment? I think my favorite definition of contentment was the one I heard during a Saturday night church service:

"When you choose what you *should* choose in the situation you *didn't* choose, you're learning contentment." Being content with being single does not mean you must ignore the desire to have a husband, but that you should *choose* to rejoice in the blessing of singleness.

> "When you choose what you should choose in the situation you didn't choose, you're learning contentment."

I won't lie and say this is easy. If you don't face enough opposition from the yearnings of your own heart, you will most certainly find conflict with people who don't understand your view on singleness. Throughout my life, I have found very few people who actually encourage me to take this time to be single, but I've found plenty who are all too eager to "help" me find a man. A couple of weeks ago, I felt like banging my head against the dinner table when someone mentioned what a "large pool of young men there must be at my church." I chuckled nervously and murmured, "Well, I guess so, but I'm really not interested," as if I were ashamed to say it. Although what I really wanted to say was, "Yes, I live in a college town where there are lots of cute guys, but I don't care because I'm not looking right now." I often find myself biting back those words, because I know people have a difficult time understanding that I'm really *not* interested in pursuing a relationship. No one seems to believe that statement can be true. They think I'm lying to myself. They think I'm in denial, while I am convinced that I am merely delaying something that God has asked me to delay for the time being.

"Surely there must be *some* young man you like," they press.

As a matter of fact, I "like" a lot of young men; I just don't understand why male/female relationships have to be romantic. I enjoy hanging out with guys in the context of friendship. Honestly, I almost prefer it over the drama that comes from spending time in a roomful of girls. Why is it that most people tend to get so caught up in the romantic aspect of relationships that they don't even realize true friendship can exist between men and women?

There are so many wonderful things about unromantic relationships. You never have to worry about breaking someone's heart or having your heart broken, you don't have to be concerned about how awkward your relationship with a guy is going to be after you've ended a romantic relationship with him, and if you truly aren't concerned with the romantic side of things, you can conduct yourself more freely in the presence of these men because you don't feel the need to impress them. When I go home to visit, I don't return to a bunch of broken hearts, but to a band of brothers. Now, I've heard it said that if every guy is your brother, you will never be able to marry one of them, and I've always wondered if whoever started that saying was trying to scare a girl away from healthy relationships with guys. The way I see it, I can only marry one man, but I can befriend them all.

FIVE YEARS AND FOREVER

Maybe you feel as if you have compromised in the area of relationships. Perhaps you have led a guy on or sacrificed your identity in order to belong to some man. Maybe, just maybe, your heart aches because you have never felt free to be yourself in a relationship. Or perhaps you feel more like our friend from *Runaway Bride* and you don't even truly know yourself. If this is the case, I want to challenge you to set aside a period of time to really get to know yourself. I want to encourage you to take a season of being dedicated to no man but Jesus.

After watching my peers bounce in and out of unhealthy dating relationships, I decided that I wanted so much more than what they had. I never wanted to find myself compromising my friendships or my standards in attempts to catch and keep some guy. And I certainly didn't want to find myself drifting further and further from God's will by becoming consumed with that one relationship. I decided that I wanted to be different than the average single girl, so I resolved not to date until my heart was firmly established in Jesus. To wait until I *knew* that I would not lose Him in trying to "keep" some guy. I gave God what I like to call "Five Years and Forever." The first five years were going to be spent making Jesus my one and only love in hopes that He would remain my first love forever.

Now before you freak out on me, I'm not saying that you have to give God five years. In fact, I'm not going to give you a time limit at all. The timing is something that is between you and God, and it is going to be different for everyone. But I highly recommend that you take at least some period of time to focus on God alone. Let Him become the Prince of your dreams, and allow Him to shape you into the woman you were meant to be.

This season of "delay" in my life is something I have not regretted in the least, and I would love for you to share in the same joy I've experienced with Jesus. At least pray about it, and ask God what He would have you to do. Don't think I'm going to be offended if you choose not to take a break from dating. Perhaps that's not where God is calling you at this specific time and place. But, if you are feeling in your heart that you *should* walk through a season of singleness, and you really don't *want* to, maybe you should pray a little harder. Regardless, there are only three people who are truly affected by your decision and, as I already stated, I am not one of them. Those three people you end up cheating—should you choose not to follow that knowing in your heart—are God, yourself and your future husband. So think about it, pray about it, and follow wherever God chooses to lead you. I promise you won't regret it.

DEALING WITH THOSE SINGLE-HATERS

As I've already warned you, the world won't understand your choice to remain unattached for a season. Some people simply won't agree that it is "necessary," while others will tell you the whole idea is downright ridiculous. Although it's widely known that I don't have a boyfriend, I try to avoid the subject of "why" because I tire of those "single-haters." You know who I mean, the ones who just "know" that you would be so happy to be introduced to their best friend's sister's favorite co-worker's second cousin three times removed... Let's face it, ladies, in a culture that is all about romantic relationships and "the heat of the moment," girls with convictions are frequently misunderstood.

Oftentimes, we feel as if we are in total seclusion from the rest of the world. This is a feeling that has most likely penetrated Christians of all generations. Turning back to the story of Esther, we read, "The girl pleased him [Hegai, the king's custodian of the harem] and won his favor. Immediately he provided her with beauty treatments and special food. He assigned to her seven maids selected from the king's palace and moved her and her maids into the best place in the harem" (Est. 2:9). Even good treatment can be seclusion at times. Hegai treated Esther like... well, like a queen, but in doing so, he secluded her from all the other girls who were competing for the crown. Even before her palace experience, Esther was a captive in a foreign land, so I'm sure there were many times in her life that she felt lonely, and perhaps even misunderstood. Sound vaguely familiar?

God never said the world would agree with you, love you, or even understand you. In fact, Jesus felt the need to point out that the world may hate you. It's right there in John 15:18-19. "If the world hates you, keep in mind that it hated me first. If you belonged to the world, it would love you as its own. As it is, you do not belong to the world, but I have chosen you out of the world. That is why the world hates you." Seems pretty harsh, huh?

If you haven't realized it already, following God isn't always easy; in fact, some days, it's downright hard. It's hard to be different from the world because there will always be a part of us that desperately wants to fit in and be accepted by everyone else. But you do not *belong* to the world; therefore, you will never *be* like the world. All you have to offer is an act. And will you ever truly feel accepted when the only thing the world will accept from you is a farce?

Before you are tempted to hang your head in despair, take heart. God wouldn't give us a message like that without tagging a little bit of hope on the end. The hope is that, though we are not accepted by the world, we have a sense of belonging in the Kingdom of Heaven. Focus in on the part of the verse that says, "I have chosen you out of the world." Did you get that? While you may be cast aside by the

> *While you may be cast aside by the world, you have been completely chosen and approved by the King of the universe.*

world, you have been completely chosen and approved by the King of the universe. I know that can be difficult to accept at times. There have been plenty of occasions throughout my life where I've voiced prayers that sounded something like this: "God, I know this world is not my home. I know I was made for heaven, and You have called me to something much greater than I can imagine, but right now, I'm just so lonely. I want to fit in. I want to belong here—now. I want to compromise, just for a moment. Just so I can imagine that I have a place here."

That's a little too painstakingly real, isn't it? But I wonder if you haven't pondered the same thing at one time or another. Let's face it, sometimes we just don't feel like walking righteously. Sometimes we just want to bend the rules a little, to give in to temptation. Sometimes we get tired of being strong. Sometimes we don't want to fight so hard. Sometimes we are tempted to agree to meet that "…second cousin three times removed…" just so we can feel like we are a part of that world.

A GRACEFUL WAITING

Let me assure you that God is all for honest confessions. You don't have to put on some "holier-than-thou" act when you bow your head in prayer. You don't have to pretend to be strong before Jesus. He knows that you struggle, and He desires for you to give Him your weaknesses so He can transform them into His strengths. After all, who better to walk through life with than the very Creator of life itself? Instead of searching for a fallible human being in whom you can confide your hopes and dreams, try talking them over with the One who breathed them into being. Let Jesus take you away from the rest of the world for a time, and allow Him to tell you who you were created to be. Invite Him to show you how you were meant to live. Let him whisper in your ear and tell you who you really are. He may tell you things like:

> *"I have loved you with an everlasting love; I have drawn you with loving-kindness."*
> ~Jeremiah 31:3

> *"Fear not, for I have redeemed you; I have summoned you by name; you are mine."*
> ~Isaiah 43:1

> *"Though the mountains be shaken and the hills removed, yet my unfailing love for you will not be shaken nor my covenant of peace be removed."*
> ~Isaiah 54:10

If you've been searching for romance, go back and read those excerpts again. The God I've become acquainted with is a total romantic. He is the author of all love stories. And these are only a few of the things He has to say to you. You will first discover His words of love to you in the Bible, but after awhile, you will begin to hear His voice with your own ears. Like the most intimate of friends, you and God will eventually develop your own little love language.

> *Like the most intimate of friends, you and God will eventually develop your own little love language.*

I encourage you to take this time that God has called you to set apart for Him, and start developing a love relationship with your true Prince. Gracefully decline any dating offers until God releases you from your commitment to love only Him. Know that you are not secluded from the entire world; just the parts of the world that are completely immersed in darkness. Go ahead and hang out with your Christian girlfriends and enjoy getting to know Christian guys as friends instead of lovers. But be careful. There is a fine line between friendship and flirting that sometimes takes awhile to firmly establish.

THE MYTH OF "CASUAL" DATING

While I'm all for cultivating healthy friendships with guys, it is wise to use discretion in your time spent with members of the opposite sex. For example, I have a friend whom we will call "Nick." After knowing Nick for quite some time, I began to get the feeling that he was beginning to develop a deeper interest in me than I had in him, so when he invited me to hang out with him one evening, I had to decline. As I was describing the scenario to a friend, she replied, "Well, he sounds like a pretty sweet guy, and you seem to get along well with him. I don't see any harm in two friends casually hanging out and maybe grabbing a cup of coffee."

Now, I'm not opposed to casually hanging out with a friend. In fact, when I went home this past Easter, I met up with a guy friend at a coffee shop, and we spent three hours catching up on everything that had happened in the six months I had been gone. But there were a few big differences in those two scenarios. For starters, Josh is perhaps one of my best friends, and I've known him for as long as I can remember. This is the guy who can read my mind and predict what I am going to say. When I'm with Josh, I don't have to worry about how he might misinterpret something I say because he *knows* me. (I mean, come on, how concerned do you have to be when your "date" looks at a storm of dark clouds blowing in and asks you if you rode in on a broom?) Secondly, when I came home from that three-hour trip, my parents weren't concerned in the least. Sure, they teased me endlessly, but they weren't truly worried because they understand our relationship. And lastly, when my mom, at the pinnacle of her teasing, announced to my entire extended family that I had just spent three hours unattended with a "young man," my cousin began pressing me for details. All I had to say was, "It was Josh," and she visibly deflated because *she* knows our relationship. But Josh is one of the few exceptions. Had I thought there was any possibility he might perceive there to be something more between us, I wouldn't have been caught dead in a coffee shop with him. Still, I generally recommend group settings where it is much harder for anyone to read hidden meanings into anything.

After watching the shipwrecks of relationships that "casual" dating has left in its wake, I'm more convinced than ever that the term itself is an oxymoron—which is why I chose not to go out with Nick that night. If I had agreed to meet him, I would have been sending mixed signals, and even if my heart would have remained completely unaffected, I'm pretty sure that his would not. This is not to say that you should completely avoid guys who show any hint of romantic interest in you. I still get along well with Nick, but we always hang out in those safe, group settings in order to avoid the "date-like" feel, and therefore, we remain friends.

Don't you remember that couple who were really good friends *until* they started dating? Then something happened, the relationship ended, and they could never go back to the way things were before they started dating. I hate that. All I can see is how they ruined a beautiful friendship, and for what—a few brief months of "romantic bliss"? Maybe I'm wrong, but I personally can't see how that would be worth the loss of a good friend. And even worse is the emotional damage that has been done. For the sake of all our guy friends out there, I'm asking you to *please* be careful with their hearts. Use discretion in your relationships, and when in doubt, turn to Jesus and ask Him what He would have you do in a particular circumstance. Then follow through with His guidance.

RELEASED IN HIS LOVE

Above all, I encourage you to take time to get to know God as you would your best friend, whether it takes twelve months, five years, or anything above, below, or in-between. I truly believe that Esther spent her required twelve months of preparation learning to fully trust in God. How else would she have devised such a clever plan to save her people? Where else would she have found the courage to appear before the king without having been summoned (an act punishable by death)? And why else would God have been the first person she turned to when her world was falling apart? I think it was natural for Esther to turn to God because her relationship with Him had already been established before she ever came to live in the palace. It became even further entrenched during her twelve months of being set apart. Secure in the love and protection of her heavenly King, Esther dared to risk the wrath of an earthly king, and in so doing, fulfilled her calling in the Kingdom-at-large.

Similarly to Esther, I challenge you to allow God to become the first Person you turn to when you are facing a dilemma. Let Him be the first One you run to when you are shouting for joy. Invite Him to take the role of a lover in your life. Give Him the heart you have been saving for your future husband. Release yourself to be touched and transformed by the love of your heavenly King. Let Him be the One who guides you through every step in life as you fulfill your calling in the Kingdom. For who knows but that you, dear sister, were made for such a time as this?

Chapter 7

Start A Revolution: Learn To Love

Waiting Defined:
Be a Waiter

"I need the painful journey of learning to love, because without it I'll remain safely encased in sterile indifference."

-Steven James

ove. That word is tossed around so casually that we aren't even sure what the *real* meaning of love is anymore. Somewhere along the line, it has taken on more definitions than it was ever meant to carry. I mean, I love God, I love my mom, I love raspberry ice cream. What exactly does that mean? Obviously I don't love ice cream in the same way I love my mom, nor do I love my mom in the same way I love my Savior. Yet I somehow expect that one word to describe the way I feel about three entirely different things. So what is the true definition of love? I wish it was as easy as grabbing a dictionary and browsing the "L's," but even the dictionary contains a few meanings that I don't believe were meant to be there. That's right; leave it to humans to legally distort the meaning of love. In order to get our mindset concerning love on the right track, we must turn to the definition given by the Creator of love itself. Let's scroll back through the pages of Scripture to find the original meaning of love.

The Bible talks about love more times than I care to even try counting. Apparently God predicted our distorted definitions and decided He needed to spell it out clearly for us. I thought a good place to start would be with the very first Bible verse we are taught in Sunday School: John 3:16. "For God so loved the world that he gave his only begotten

Son, that whoever believes in him shall not perish but have eternal life." I know, I know, you've heard that verse a thousand times. You probably repeated it verbatim with me. But have you ever truly thought about what it means? Have you ever really considered the impli-

> *Love, true love, is sacrifice.*

cations that verse contains? God loved, God gave, and Jesus *died*. Love—true love—is sacrifice.

Fairytale author, Hans Christian Andersen, never married, but I think he understood love better than most of us. He seemed to realize that love often comes hand-in-hand with pain. Take the story of *The Little Mermaid*, for example. Andersen's original version does not contain the happy ending Disney portrays. Although the prince acknowledges that the Little Mermaid's devotion to him is "great and sincere," he never returns her affection. He never realizes the true depths of her love. He never learns that she had risked her life in order to save him after he had been cast from his ship one stormy night at sea. He never discovers that she had kept his lifeless body afloat all that dreadful night as the waves slowly carried them to shore. He never finds out that she had sacrificed the gift of speech in order to be with him. He never realizes that every step she took felt like walking on knives— that all the dances she danced to please him caused her unimaginable pain. He remains forever unaware of her agony as she willingly bore every trial out of love for him. And even though the prince is completely oblivious to all these things, the Little Mermaid loved him with everything that she was.

Surely she did not think he would come to love her as deeply as she loved him. Perhaps she *hoped* that this would happen, but I'm not convinced she *believed* that it would. He had already made it clear that there was a different woman in his life—the woman he believed had saved his life on the night of the shipwreck. Still, the Little Mermaid loved him, without expecting anything in return—without believing he would eventually relieve her of her pain. She gave him everything she had... even her life. She had taken a gamble when she told an old sea witch that she would earn the prince's love in three days or forfeit her life. And when her time was up and she was given the option of living—if only she would take the prince's life—the Little Mermaid cast herself into the sea. She willingly sacrificed herself to an awful fate so that the one she loved, quite literally more than life itself, might live in peace.

Sadly, the prince never knew what he had missed, but I would be willing to bet he was never loved so deeply again in his life. Most people don't love like the Little Mermaid. Most people don't give *everything* they have to give. I am inspired by the way she loved. The thing I find most fascinating about her story is that she *knew* what her love would cost her before she traded her fins for feet. She *knew* that she would no longer be able to speak or sing or shout. She *knew* that every step she took on land would feel as if a thousand needles were poking into her feet. The sea witch had warned her of the pain she would endure. Still, she chose to love the prince no matter what it would cost her.

I think back to a relationship in my own life that caused me a tremendous amount of grief. While I hadn't literally sacrificed my voice or walked in pain as the Little Mermaid had, when the relationship ended suddenly and tragically, I was too stunned to speak and almost *felt* as if someone had plunged a dagger into my heart. Had I known, at the start of our relationship, the pain this person would cause me in the years to come, I must confess that I probably would not have let myself love that person so freely. But looking back, I'm glad that I didn't know those details in the beginning or I might not have loved as deeply as I did... and I would have missed out on a beautiful thing. Although the pain was—and sometimes still is—all too real, I've learned that it is *always* worth it to love.

> *It is always worth it to love.*

LOVE IS MORE THAN JUST A FAIRYTALE

Perhaps you aren't content to take a fictional story and apply it to real life. After all, storybook heroes can do anything. Of course the Little Mermaid can portray the perfect ideal of love. That's all she is—an ideal. A figment of someone's imagination. Love doesn't really happen the way it is written in fairytales. No matter how much we "wish upon a star," our dreams of true love do not come true.

Or do they? Take the Biblical example of Jacob and Rachel for starters. Here's a real-life fairytale for you. Jacob struck up a deal with Rachel's father, promising that he would work for seven years in exchange for Rachel's hand in marriage. Read Genesis 29:20 and tell me if you've ever heard a more romantic statement: "So Jacob served seven years to get Rachel, but they seemed like only a few days to him because of his love for her." I think that sounds like something straight out of a fairytale. Seven years of hard work meant nothing to Jacob because no irritation that his work could present would ever rival his love for Rachel. And even when he was deceived and forced to serve an additional seven years to win Rachel as his bride, he did so out of his great love for her.

Lest you think this is the only example, one can also learn from the apostle Paul. Listen to what he tells us in Philippians 2:17-18: "But even if I am poured out like a drink offering on the sacrifice and service coming from your faith, I am glad and rejoice with all of you. So you too should be glad and rejoice with me."

I'm sorry, what did he just say? Being "poured out like a drink offering" doesn't sound too pleasant to me, and yet, Paul said he was happy about it. That is love right there—giving until it hurts, bending until it breaks, pouring until it is empty and dry... and believing the pain was worth it in the end.

Love is hard. It goes against our sinful, prideful nature. We don't want to pour all our time and energy into the well-being of someone else; we're too concerned with our own needs. We don't want to take time to truly see someone else; we want to be noticed ourselves. We don't want to be like the Little Mermaid who gave, and gave, and gave, and was never thanked or even acknowledged. We love only if someone is willing to love us in return, but true love is not inhibited by such conditions. True love is *unconditional*.

I have a friend who is a nurse in the ICU. She literally saves lives every day by the seemingly simple things she does. But people seldom appreciate her efforts. She is rarely thanked for her service because most don't seem to realize just how important her job actually is. She confesses that sometimes she feels like she needs to be applauded for the good things she does, but what would happen if she took offense to the fact that few seemed grateful? What would happen if she chose not to help anyone who didn't acknowledge the wonderful work she was doing? Let's just say that if I were going to undergo a drastic surgery, I would have the procedure done in a different hospital.

You can't stop saving lives simply because the person you saved may never thank you. What about the paramedics who rescue people when they are unconscious? Those victims aren't even going to *know* who rescued them. They might pass their savior on the streets or in the grocery store and never realize the debt they owe him. Hmm. Sounds sort of like a fairytale I once read...

Jesus was familiar with ungratefulness as well. Luke 17:12-19 tells us of a time He healed ten men from leprosy, but only one came back to thank Him. In fact, Jesus healed a lot of people who probably never thanked Him, but their ungratefulness didn't stop Him from lavishing love on those who needed it most. He still chose to die for humankind even if most of our race would never acknowledge His existence.

LOVE IS A KING DISGUISED AS A SERVANT

Our seventh and final definition of *wait* is *"be a waiter."* Once again, it's not a very exciting definition, but this one is necessary. This one is not only a definition of the word *wait*, but a commandment from God. Jesus shared this command in Mark 10:42-45. "Jesus called them [the disciples] together and said, 'You know that those who are regarded as rulers of the Gentiles lord it over them, and their high officials exercise authority over them. Not so with you. Instead, whoever wants to become great among you must be your servant, and whoever wants to be first must be slave of all. For even the Son of Man did not come to be served, but to serve, and to give his life as a ransom for many.'"

Jesus presents Himself as the perfect example of a servant. He was willing to lay down His life for those He loved; yet so many of us are unwilling to give up even a simple comfort. We aren't willing to take the backseat. We want to make life all about us, but Jesus offers the ultimate paradox: The truly great are servants; not kings. And if you want to be "number one," you must make yourself "number zero." It really doesn't make any sense, but I've always figured that if God made sense to the human mind, He wouldn't be God. Logically, it doesn't make sense that Jesus came to earth to die for our sins, either. He could have come down and taken the world by force. He could have brought His legions of angels to fight against the oppressors and tyrants of the earth. But Jesus didn't do this. The only weapon He bore was love.

God knew that our world didn't need saved from the evil rulers of the day. He knew that each evil ruler would only be replaced by another... and another and another. He came to demonstrate love because love would bring the ultimate change in this world.

Last summer, I spent a long weekend with a friend. Her precious two-year-old son liked to play rough, and he came up to me a couple times and hit me as hard as he could. Whenever he did this, his mom or dad would pull him aside and say, "No, *love* the niña."

At first, I thought this was a rather strange way of correcting him (and not because it was in Spanish; I had grown used to that). Most people would say something more along the lines of, "No, we don't hit people." But instead of being told not to hit, he was taught to love. Why? Because love has no desire to harm.

My friend could have told her son that it wasn't right to hit people, and he might spend his life restraining himself from punching someone in the face simply because it was the right thing to do. Or, he could learn to love and lose all desire to hit someone in the first place. "Love the niña" was a long-term answer.

LOVE STARTS A REVOLUTION, ONE LIFE AT A TIME

Love is revolutionary. God's love transforms lives. God commands us to love one another because love is the most important of all His commandments.

Love is revolutionary.

> One of the teachers of the law came and heard them debating. Noticing that Jesus had given them a good answer, he asked him, "Of all the commandments, which is the most important?"
>
> "The most important one," answered Jesus, "is this: 'Hear, O Israel, the Lord our God, the Lord is one. Love the Lord your God with all your heart and with all your soul and with all your mind and with all your strength.' The second is this: 'Love your neighbor as yourself.' There is no commandment greater than these."
>
> "Well said, teacher," the man replied. "You are right in saying that God is one and there is no other but him. To love him with all your heart, with all your understanding and with all your strength, and to love your neighbor as yourself is more important than all burnt offerings and sacrifices."
>
> When Jesus saw that he had answered wisely, he said to him, "You are not far from the kingdom of God." And from then on no one dared ask him any more questions (Mark 12:28-34).

I've heard that many people have a hard time reading the Old Testament. They find it boring, not culturally relevant, and/or difficult to understand. I find it fascinating. Without the Old Testament, the New Testament really makes no sense. While some people tend to write it off as "just a bunch of old laws," I find that those "old laws" are what make the above passage so liberating. In this passage from Mark, Jesus doesn't *eliminate* the laws of the Old Testament; He *explains* them. By clearly stating that these are the two most important commandments, He allows all the others to simply fall into place. A world full of love is a world without hate. And a world without hate is a world without violence, sin, and pain. A world where love reigns is paradise. If the world were to learn to love once more, we might be restored to something similar to the former glory of Eden. But our world has become so twisted by hatred and distorted by sin that we do not even recognize love anymore.

Jesus came to earth for a season, gave His life as the ultimate expression of love, and left behind a legacy—a promise that love would continue. He spent three years pouring Himself into twelve men, teaching them to serve, commanding them to love so that the world might be transformed by that same love that the Messiah so openly displayed.

Likewise, you have a task to carry out. Whether single, married, widowed or divorced, this is a command that stretches through the ages. "A new command I give you: Love one another. As I have loved you, so you must love one another. By this all men will know that you are my disciples, if you love one another" (John 13:34-35). Hmm... do you think maybe Jesus wanted us to love one another? Of course you and I are called to love, because this is how the world will see that we are followers of God. This is how the world will realize that there is hope in this lifetime.

LOVE IS ALWAYS WORTH IT

I suppose when most Christians are asked to define love, they turn to the familiar Bible passage in 1 Corinthians 13:4-7. "Love is patient, love is kind. It does not envy, it does not boast, it is not proud. It is not rude, it is not self-seeking, it is not easily angered, it keeps no record of wrongs. Love does not delight in evil but rejoices with the truth. It always protects, always trusts, always hopes, always perseveres."

Personally, I like the three verses leading up to that passage: "If I speak in the tongues of men and of angels, but have not love, I am only a resounding gong or a clanging cymbal. If I have the gift of prophecy and can fathom all mysteries and all knowledge, and if I have a faith that can move mountains, but have not love, I am nothing. If I give all I possess to the poor and surrender my body to the flames, but have not love, I gain nothing."

You could accomplish all your wildest dreams and find that they were for naught. You could become the most famous, wealthy, revered, and admired person on the planet, and find that you are still unsatisfied. A life lived without love is scarcely a life at all; it's a mere existence. There is a big difference between living and existing.

I have a friend who has been hurt many times in her life. Because of all those times she has been failed, she is afraid to open her heart and trust again. One time, I playfully asked her if she would be my friend. I wasn't prepared for her gravely serious response. "All right, we'll give it a shot," she said. "But if you hurt me, we're through. Because I've been hurt before, and I don't want to be hurt by you. Got it?"

I blinked, surprised by her little outburst. Then I breathed her name softly and replied, "I can't promise I won't hurt you because sometimes I do stupid things. But I can promise that I will try as hard as I can not to hurt you. And if I do fail you, I'm going to be more upset with myself than you'll be."

She apparently wasn't prepared for my response either, because she hesitated before answering. "Cool, that's all I need."

It is for people like these that we must learn to love with everything we've got. It is for the hurting and broken, the wounded and betrayed, that we must prove that love is more than a feeling—more than a fantasy. If love means sacrifice, then sacrifice we must. If God could come down from heaven in order to walk the earth in human form, lavish love upon those who wouldn't accept it, heal people who wouldn't be grateful, wash the feet of the man who would hand Him over to be killed, and willingly give His life for the people who were screaming, "Crucify!" then we can certainly sacrifice our time, our comfort, and our selfish desires. We may have to endure a bit of pain, suffer through some heartache, and shed a few tears. Somewhat like the Little Mermaid, we may have to forfeit our voice, in order to listen with our ears. We may feel the prick of a thousand needles poking into our hearts when we watch someone we love go though a difficult time. We may have to give until it hurts, bend until we break, and pour out until we are dry, but if we have loved truly, we will find that it will be worth it in the end. Love is *always* worth it in the end.

Chapter 8

The Search For Significance

"It is not the truth you know but the truth you live that sets you free."

-Lisa Bevere

Every girl longs for a happily ever after, but few actually believe her dreams can come true. We live in a world filled with sin and pain and say to ourselves, "My life is *nothing* like a fairytale." It's funny how we only see what we want to see. The happy ending. The princess with her prince. Once the victory has been won, it's easy to forget the pain and the struggles. But think about it…

Cinderella was a servant in her own house, despised by her stepsisters. Snow White fled into the forest because her stepmother had a hit out on her. Rapunzel spent most of her life locked away in a tower because the woman she believed was her mother was actually a selfish, old witch. Face it, girlfriend, the fairytale characters we know and love didn't exactly live lives of ease. They, too, faced struggle and heartache and tears before they ever tasted the triumph of "happily ever after."

The fairytale heroines offer a sign of hope. Though their stories are different, their determination is the same. Each of them has a dream, and they will stop at nothing to fulfill it. They triumph through the pain and the trials and the tears because their dreams propel them. That's the main difference between the young women of today and the storybook heroines we loved as children. The fairytale characters have not allowed themselves to become jaded by the world in which they live, unlike so many of us who have lost the magic of "once upon a time." We've grown up and forgotten how to experience the wonder of Neverland. We've come to believe that faith, trust and pixie dust is a farce, that "second star to the right and straight on 'til morning" are impossible directions, and that there is no world beyond the reality in which we are living. But we are wrong. So maybe there are no islands with pirates and mermaids and fairies, but there is an unseen realm in this world that holds castles and angels and wonder. Even though we may *know* that in our heads, we still find it hard to *believe* in our hearts.

We were born with a yearning for the fairytales—a dream of a bright future. But somewhere amidst the heartache and disappointment, we lose that yearning. And instead of mourning our lost sense of wonder, we simply claim that we've "grown up." We accept our loss of hope as an inevitable step into reality, but it was never meant to be that way. When Jesus came and walked the earth, He instructed us to become like little children. I think this was an invitation to recapture the magic and wonder of the fairytale. *His* fairytale.

It seems ironic that many people place God in a category with unicorns, fairies, and other fantastical creatures. After all, what God offers us is not an escape from reality but the chance to stop playing make-believe. He extends to us the opportunity to drop our pretenses and truly be ourselves for a change. We don't ever have to worry that He won't accept us as we are, so we can put away the masks behind which we attempt to hide. He sees right through those masks anyway, however elaborate they may be. And you know what? He loves the girl behind the disguise, because she's the girl He created.

> *In a world of broken promises and shattered dreams, God offers you a chance to start over.*

In a world of broken promises and shattered dreams, God offers you a chance to start over. To stop playing pretend and to embrace the person you were meant to be. So why are you holding back?

RELEASING THE LIES

Inside each of us is a desire to be desired, a longing to be loved, and a yearning to be significant. What does this have to do with Beyond Waiting? Absolutely everything.

I don't have to tell you that ours is a culture that lives for relationships. By the time we are teens, we are all too familiar with the theory that our lives are not complete without our "other half." The search for Prince Charming is a search for significance more than anything else. Because we don't believe that we are complete in ourselves, we set out in search of someone who will fill that void in our hearts. We convince ourselves that only when we find "the one" will we truly be happy. Unfortunately, we are looking for fulfillment in all the wrong places.

I fully believe that we will never be able to move Beyond Waiting until we move beyond believing that our worth is determined by man. We can't spend the rest of our lives thinking that a ring on our finger is what gives us significance. Relationships are definitely meant to be a good thing. After all, God did say that it's not good for man to be alone. But it's also not good for two people to get so wrapped up in each other that they lose all sense of self. So learn to be content where you are, no matter what your relationship status happens to be. Even more importantly, be content with *who* you are.

I think it's safe to say that most girls aren't satisfied with themselves. There's a reason for our discontent, you know. We've been fed lies all of our lives—from the television, the magazines, and sometimes our own families. I've known girls whose parents have told them that they're stupid and will never amount to anything. Others have been told they'll never be as pretty as/ smart as/you-name-it-as their sisters. That's hard stuff to take from your parents. The worst part is that it's not even true. These girls should never have had to suffer that verbal abuse. And neither should you.

I don't care what you've been told, your life *is* of value. Regardless of what you've been made to falsely believe, you were created for a purpose. If you've been called ugly, stupid, worthless, or anything else of the like, it's a lie from the pit of hell. God doesn't make mistakes; He creates masterpieces. The first step in embracing your significance is releasing the lies you've carried far too long.

You *are* beautiful. You *are* loved. You are strong and smart and full of potential. And I have scripture to back it up. Read on, fair maiden…

YOU ARE BEAUTIFUL

Perhaps you've heard the statement, "Disney gave me unrealistic expectations of men." Well, here's a good one for you: Hollywood gave me unrealistic expectations of body image. The pixilated perfection every girl feels the need to achieve is causing far more damage than Disney's extraordinary heroes ever did.

The culture in which we live has selected an impossible image and declared it beautiful, leaving the rest of us to mourn the fact that we are too fat, too skinny, too short, too tall, too… too… you name it. But when God created the world—and that includes when He designed *you*—He said that all He had made was good. But what exactly does that mean?

For most of my life, I thought I was merely "good enough." I'd throw on a pair of jeans and a t-shirt, run a brush through my hair, and tell the image in the mirror, "Eh, God said that it was good." But I never thought myself beautiful. Not to God, not to anyone.

But what I failed to think about, even as I quoted that verse from Genesis, is that the Bible doesn't say:

"God created a size-fourteen, average-looking woman with brown hair and dull brown eyes, and said that she was good. Then He created a size-zero, stunningly attractive blond with sparkling blue eyes and said that she was better." Go ahead and search your Bible from cover to cover. You won't find it in there. But you might find a few other verses that will transform the way you view yourself. Psalm 45:11 struck a deep chord in my heart. "The king is enthralled by your beauty; honor him, for he is your lord."

God? Enthralled by *my* beauty? No. There's not much to be enthralled by. But if that wasn't enough to leave me breathless, imagine my surprise when I read Song of Songs 4:7. "All beautiful you are, my darling; there is no flaw in you."

All right, now we're just getting ridiculous. No flaws? Do I need to start listing them? But between those two verses, the truth is revealed. I find that God is enthralled by my flawless beauty.

I can hear your objections already. You're probably pointing to your most despised feature and saying, "This is most definitely a flaw!" Hey, I'm not exactly proud of the perpetual bags under my eyes, but I know that God put them there on purpose. I can only surmise that this means He likes them—even though I can't begin to explain why.

To say that one person is the perfect image of beauty is like saying that my favorite color is green, therefore all other colors are ugly. If we were to judge the color purple based on how green it is, we would never appreciate it for its beauty. In similar manner, you can't compare yourself to anyone else and still see yourself as the marvelous master-piece God created. If God is inspired enough to make each snowflake differently than the next, why would we expect Him to make carbon-copy people? You, girl, are a designer original—cut from a different cloth and shaped into a different pattern than anyone else on the planet. That's something to be proud of!

> *You can't compare yourself to anyone else and still see yourself as the marvelous masterpiece God created.*

So there I was, "good enough/merely passable" me, standing in front of a mirror when it dawned on me for the first time… I'm beautiful. That may sound silly and possibly even a bit vain, but that's how it happened. I stared dumbfounded at my reflection for a moment and spoke the thought aloud, as if the sound of my voice would make it a reality. "I'm beautiful."

God wants you to experience that same beauty-awaking. It's time to make friends with the girl in the mirror. Ask God to give you His eyes, and try telling your reflection that you're beautiful. If you say it enough, you'll soon start to believe it.

YOU ARE LOVED

I have a confession to make. Sometimes I scoff at the basic truths of Christianity. Not that I don't believe them, but simply because I've heard them so many times. Those of you who were raised in church can probably relate. I mean, really, how many times do you need to hear the words, "Jesus loves you"?

Lately I've come to think that the reminder might not be a bad thing because, while I know the truth in my head, I sometimes forget to let it sink into my heart. There are days that I don't truly believe Jesus loves me. Though I hear it time and time again, I don't let it reach into the depths of my soul and transform me from the inside out. Sometimes I move to the rhythm of faith completely out of habit rather than passion.

I sang the words, "Yes, Jesus loves me," for fourteen years before I truly started believing it. I knew it in my head, but not in my heart. I feel that's where most of us are in our walks with God. It's all about how much we know *about* God, instead of how much we've personally encountered Him.

When I finally got a glimpse of the God described in Zephaniah 3:17—the One who rejoices over me with singing—my life was turned upside down. That's a powerful verse, you know. If you've read through the Bible like a textbook, never noticing the romance of God, I'd encourage you to look that one up. It says that God is with you. That He saves you and takes great delight in you. That He quiets you with His love. It's a beautiful, romantic picture of the God we often think isn't taking an active role in our lives.

Over and over, the Bible references God's love. From Genesis to Revelation, God is recorded as wooing His bride. And throughout that same length of text, His chosen people are shown rejecting His love. It's absolutely heartbreaking, but I know I'm guilty of the same crime. When the Bible tells me that God has loved me with an everlasting love (Jer. 31:3), I'm not even moved. I can wake up and read that I'm far more valuable than the sparrows God cares for (Matt. 6:26), but in my heart I believe that I'm only as valuable as the next cutting remark someone makes about me.

I love the scene in *Princess Diaries* when Mia invites Michael to the ball. After pursuing a guy who only wanted to use her, she turns back to the guy who has loved her all along. When he asks her why she chose him as the date to her special event, she replies simply: "Because you loved me when I was invisible."

We're a lot more like Mia Thermopolis than we care to admit. How many times have we pursued the wrong lover, only to find ourselves crawling back to God's arms in the end? But the beautiful thing is that God *does* love us when we're invisible. He loves us when we feel ugly and unlovable and alone in the world. When everyone else has failed us, His love still stands.

Romans 8:38-39 says, "For I am convinced that neither death nor life, neither angels nor demons, neither the present nor the future, nor any powers, neither height nor depth, nor anything else in all creation, will be able to separate us from the love of God that is in Christ Jesus our Lord."

That verse ought to give you goose bumps. Unconditional love is hard to come by in this world, yet God lavishes it unsparingly on every undeserving human being that ever walked the planet. Though you may feel unloved, invisible, and insignificant, one drop of the Savior's blood is enough to erase all those insecurities that have plagued you thus far.

I pray for you the very same prayer Paul recorded in the book of Ephesians: "that you, being rooted and established in love, may have the power, together with all the saints, to grasp how wide and long and high and deep is the love of Christ, and to know this love that surpasses knowledge—that you may be filled to the measure of all the fullness of God" (Eph. 3:17b-19).

YOU ARE STRONG

When I hear the word "strength," a woman is not the first thing that comes to mind. I think of a football player, a body builder, my dad's calloused, carpenter hands. That's why I find it interesting that this "not-your-typical-girly-word" is found in the definition of the Proverbs 31 woman. "She is clothed with strength and dignity; she can laugh at the days to come" (vs. 25).

If I thought it was interesting that the word "strength" was in there at all, I find it even more interesting that it's coupled with dignity and the ability to laugh. Apparently, those three things are a package deal. I love the idea of coupling strength with laughter, perhaps because I'm prone to fits of laughter—often at things that truly aren't that funny. I think I often laugh just to keep myself from crying. But really, it takes a strong woman to smile in the face of an uncertain future. It takes a strong woman to decide that she's going to be joyful no matter what the day may hold. It takes a strong woman to hold her head high when her entire world is crumbling around her.

You are strong if you refuse to let the trials of life beat you down. You are strong if you can accept the criticism of others and not let it destroy your self-esteem. You are strong if you can walk through life without needing the approval of another human being.

But you must be careful that your strength never turns to hardness. Strength is a good trait; hardness is not. Hardness portrays many of the same traits as strength, but while strength comes from embracing the freedom Jesus offers, hardness comes from closing yourself off to the world. Strength is when you rest secure in the fact that you are significant; hardness is when you are afraid to allow yourself to trust.

Perhaps the true reason Proverbs 31:25 couples strength with laughter is to remind us that the strong woman is free to laugh. She's not bitter, closed off and wounded; but loving, open and redeemed.

YOU ARE SMART

"You're so stupid. Why are you so stupid?"

I cringed at the words, and I wasn't even their intended target. While the cutting words that spewed from her father's lips made my friend cower, they incited rage within me. I wanted to stand up and scream, "No, you're stupid!" Because I knew the truth.

My friend is a beautiful, lovable, strong, intelligent young woman, and nothing she could have done was deserving of such a scathing statement.

Our culture relies too much on book smarts. If you didn't get an "A" on your history exams, you must be pretty dumb. But memorization skills aren't an accurate measure of intelligence. I managed to get "A's" in science, but when my scientist friend starts talking equations and formulas, I realize exactly how little that "A" means. I could pass the test, but I can't perform an experiment. Does that mean I'm dumb? No. It simply means I should leave science to the scientists and stick to writing.

Intelligence comes in different forms. I can work wonders with words, but don't ask me to solve a formula, compose a song, or explain to you how plants grow. I can't do it. I don't think that way. The conflict comes when we start comparing ourselves to another person and think that we're not smart unless we're able to do what they do. After finding myself continually falling into the "I-wish-I-had-that-gift" mindset, I wrote this poem to remind myself that my gift matters:

> *If I were an artist,*
> *I'd take my paints and create*
> *A glorious sunset.*
> *I'd duplicate the image my Father made for me*
> *On the canvas of the sky.*
> *I'd set it in a background of red and pink*
> *Dusted with traces of yellow and orange,*

As the sun rises over the mountains
And penetrates the realm of darkness
With the glory of its light.
But I don't have the ability
To change colors into beauty.
And so I'll cling to my passion
Because I, I paint with words.

I wrote three more stanzas where I remind myself that I do the same thing with drawing, dancing and music. My gifts are different from the talents I listed in my poem, but they serve the same purpose: They are all a form of worship, and they all reflect the glory of the Creator in His marvelous, artistic intelligence.

YOU ARE FULL OF POTENTIAL

One verse that blows me out of the water is found in the opening chapter of Jeremiah: "Before I formed you in the womb I knew you, before you were born I set you apart; I appointed you as a prophet to the nations" (Jer. 1:5).

Wait. God knew me even *before* I was born? Did He know the year I would make my appearance on earth? Did He have my family all picked out for me? Does this mean that there's a purpose for my whole entire life? Does this mean that my existence is teeming with potential? Because that's what it sounds like to me. I mean, if God knew Jeremiah was going to be one of the most beloved Biblical prophets, surely He knows exactly what He created Rebekah Snyder for. Surely He knows exactly what He created *you* for.

This idea is reinforced in Psalm 139: "My frame was not hidden from you when I was made in the secret place. When I was woven together in the depths of the earth, your eyes saw my unformed body. All the days ordained for me were written in your book before one of them came to be" (vs. 15-16).

I'm of the belief that God doesn't waste words. If He took the time to write every single day of your life in a book, you can bet that He has weaved an amazing plot into the pages of your life. God dreams big dreams for His children, and the potential He placed in you at birth is simply unimaginable.

> God dreams big dreams for His children, and the potential He placed in you at birth is simply unimaginable.

TOO GOOD TO BE TRUE

"Really?" you ask. *"Can this really be true? Why would God care about my life?"* That's a question I find hard to answer. It's mind-boggling to think that the God who created the universe actually cares about us. It's crazy to believe that the God who makes the flowers grow every spring has actually taken time to count the number of hairs on my head. In a world of

sunshine and mountains, oceans and planets—a world where more than six billion people live and breathe, God still cares about the itty-bitty details of our lives. Now *that's* significance.

Even David, a man after God's own heart, struggled with this concept, as evidence by Psalm 8:3-4: "When I consider your heavens, the work of your fingers, the moon and the stars, which you have set in place, what is man that you are mindful of him, the son of man that you care for him?"

David never provided an answer for that question, and I don't claim to know more than he did. I honestly don't know why God cares about us. But I know that He does. And therefore, every single moment of your life matters.

That's why Beyond Waiting is such an important concept to grasp. We're wasting the years that God has granted us if we remain consumed by this fascination with earthly relationships. The real journey of Beyond Waiting is much more than that. It's about finding your way home to the heart of the Father. This book isn't about me, it isn't about men, it isn't about relationships; it's about you and the God who created you for a purpose. It's about discovering that purpose and living with passion. I'm not talking about "finding yourself" as the world likes to say. I'm talking about letting yourself be found.

You, princess, are being pursued. The Father from whom you were taken at birth has never stopped searching for you. It's the greatest fairytale of all time, and that is why so many are hesitant to believe in it. Those of us who have lost our sense of wonder have ceased believing in the impossibilities of the story of God. But as a friend's quote reminds me, "God is very much alive and really, really awesome." I know this for a fact, and I hope you know it too.

CONCLUSION

Happily Ever After

"And while Cinderella and her prince
did live happily ever after, the point,
gentlemen, is that they lived."

-Ever After

Once upon a time, there was a young maiden who wondered how, time and time again, her neighbor refused the offer to join her and her friends on their little adventures. *Waiting for Prince Charming*, she claimed. Well, *this* young maiden didn't have time to simply *wait*. She had dreams to fulfill, adventures to live, and a whole, wide world to explore.

She and her friends were on their way to the marketplace where they would examine the new wares that had been imported from distant lands. The bazaar was a flurry of colors and motion as men and women from all stations of life gathered to observe the season's newest fashions. The young maiden and her friends "oohed" and "ahhed" over the exotic garments. Though none of them could afford such luxuries, they still enjoyed holding the lavish dresses against their chests, imagining what it might be like to attend a ball wearing such delicate gowns.

The excited girls wandered from stall to stall, admiring the bobbles and bangles fashioned with gems and beads from remote islands. Inhaling the sights and sounds, they embraced the world through the unique and varied offerings of the marketplace. The scent of roasting meat led them to a booth where enticing foods were being cooked. As they sampled the spices of the

Orient and tasted succulent sweets from the Arabian Peninsula, the young maiden realized that this may be the closest she would ever come to traveling the world, and she was determined to savor every moment.

Not until after having explored every square inch of the bazaar did the young friends run off to enjoy a picnic at a nearby meadow. They talked excitedly of all the things they had seen—of dreams, and of distant lands, and of princes. Though the daisy chains they fashioned and weaved throughout each other's hair that day were temporary, the memories they formed would last a lifetime.

When spring faded into summer, the young maiden joined her friends for yet another adventure. This time they journeyed through the forest to their favorite lake. Stripping down to their petticoats, they jumped into the water, splishing and splashing to their hearts' content. Once convinced that their hands could be mistaken for prunes, the young women climbed out of the water and began picking blackberries from nearby bushes as they waited for their garments to dry.

The young maiden barely seemed to catch her breath before the leaves on the trees transformed into brilliant shades of red and gold, announcing to the world that autumn had arrived. Now she had time to think of nothing but the preparations for the Harvest Festival. She knew all of the hard work would be nearly forgotten once the games and festivities had begun. For a moment, she wondered what it would be like to share this glorious season with the prince of her dreams, but

Happily Ever After   159

her thoughts were interrupted by her friend's invitation to watch the children break the piñata. Oh well. Perhaps one day he would be there to share in her joy, but she had little time to think of it now. After all, there was a celebration taking place at this moment, and she had no intention of missing out on it.

The fading colors signified that winter was well on its way. The young maiden held her breath in anticipation. Small snowflakes had already begun fluttering throughout the sky. Perhaps tonight would be the night of the big snowfall! She thought of the delight it would be to wake up to a world blanketed in a thick, white coating of snow. If the snows came, she would spend the whole next day sledding with her friends. They would play in the frosty wonderland until they could no longer feel their toes. Then they would return to the fireside to warm themselves while sipping mugs of steaming cider.

The years rushed by in similar fashion, each season bringing new adventures of its own. It was all the young maiden could do to grasp each moment as it flew by. One particular harvest season, she found herself spinning on the dance floor, the music coursing through her veins and inspiring her every move. As the tempo increased, she spun faster and faster and faster… until she collided with the body of a young man. "Oh, I'm sorry," the young maiden exclaimed, struggling to catch her balance.

"It's quite all right," the man smiled, cocking his head to the side. "Have I seen you somewhere before?"

"I don't know," the young maiden replied. "I suppose it's possible."

"I'm pretty sure I have seen you," the young man resolved. "Although it's probably been awhile as I've been traveling the world the past couple of years."

"Oh really? Where have you been?" the maiden wondered aloud.

The man told of his travels to faraway lands. He spoke of cultures and creatures of which the young maiden had only dreamed. "And where have you been, my fair maiden?" he asked once he had finished his tale.

"Mostly around here," she shrugged. "My friends and I find that the market is the closest we will ever come to exploring the world. We have picnics in the meadow, swim in the lake, and pick flowers and black-berries as we enjoy one another's company. I suppose our silly excursions don't seem all that exciting to someone like you, but I've enjoyed them immensely. Especially these dances at the Harvest Festival."

"Well then, please," the handsome young man implored, "don't let me interrupt you." And with that statement, he extended his hand and invited her to dance. And as she took his hand and stepped onto the dance floor, she skipped right over "happily ever after" and embraced a whole new chapter of "once upon a time."

An Invitation to the Palace

Perhaps you aren't familiar with the fairytale that began all fairytales. Perhaps the story of the cross has never come alive to you. Perhaps you still see God as some cosmic force that resides in outer space and has no part in your life today. I understand. I was raised in church, but God didn't come to life for me until I was fourteen years old and read Shannon Kubiak Primicerio's interpretation of a God who dances.

If you're looking for something that will rock your world, allow me to introduce you to the God of the fairytales:

Once upon a time, God created the heavens and the earth. With a single breath, He made the stars, the air, the seas. When God spoke, antelope burst to life, leaping through the safari; fish exploded into being, dancing through the coral reefs in a flash of color. God looked at what He had created and said that it was good. Then He did something He had never done before. He got down in the dirt and began to shape it into a masterpiece. He could have spoken as He had before, but He didn't. Because this creation was different. This creation was special. This creation was formed in the very image of the Most High.

But this creation—human, as it's called—strayed from the Creator. God's special masterpiece turned its back on the Most High, disobeying His commands. And, in doing so, it did the one thing no other creation had been given the power to do… It broke God's heart.

But did God remain bitter? No. Did He cast aside His prized creation for all eternity? Certainly not. With a whisper through the ages, He begged them to return to Him. Time and time again, humankind betrayed Him, abandoning themselves in the arms of other lovers. Yet God continued to welcome them back with open arms.

But eventually their sins became too many. The chasm grew too wide. The distance between God and His creation was too vast a gap for any man to bridge. But God wanted His creation to be with Him once more, so He offered the final sacrifice. He sent His Son to die, knowing that this demonstration of love would be the only thing powerful enough to reunite heaven and earth.

This is the fairytale that inspired all other fairytales. There was a King who yearned for the end of a curse, a Prince who was willing to sacrifice His very life for His beloved, and a love that would prove stronger than death.

The story of our world in a nutshell is that God created, God loved, and Jesus died. It doesn't make sense, but then... Fairytales rarely do. Why does the prince marry the peasant? Why does Beauty fall in love with the beast? Why does a Lover surrender His life in hopes that His beloved will be restored to Him?

If you've never experienced the magic of this real-life fairytale, consider this your invitation to the palace. The Prince of Heaven surrendered His life in order to spend eternity with you. And all we humans have to do to receive the restoration Jesus offered is simply believe that He came, died to save us, and rose again, because death was not strong enough to conquer His love. All we have to do is thank Him for His sacrifice and ask Him to include us in His divine story.

I hope to see you at the palace someday.

Study Guide

This Study Guide is meant to be used for group discussion or personal reflection in hopes that the questions and thoughts therein will spur you to pick up a pen and begin writing, rewriting, or editing the story of your life. God has plans for you to live an abundant and full life, but that exhilarating contentment is only found as you abide in His love and purposes for your life.

INTRODUCTION:
Writing Your Story

Story Lines

If you are finding that your story is all too similar to that of the maiden in our introduction, I want to challenge you to stop staring out at the horizon. Stop fantasizing that today might be the day. Instead, begin taking steps in the direction that will lead you beyond your what-ifs.

Word Search

"I have told you these things, that my joy and delight may be in you, and that your joy and gladness may be of full measure and complete and overflowing."

~John 15:11 (Amp.)

Writing Your Story:

+ Do you ever allow your longings for a
  husband to override your present-day
  goals or dreams?

+ What do you think makes the village girls
  able to actively enjoy life as it happens?
  Would you have a hard time joining
  them? Why or why not?

+ What do you suppose the prince will think
  when he realizes that the young maiden
  has merely been waiting… and waiting…
  and waiting… for his arrival?

+ Do you think that your life, as of this
  moment, is one that is developing and
  growing you? If not, what are some things
  that you can do to help yourself become
  more engaged in life? (And sorry, sister,
  I'm not talking about the ring-on-your-
  finger style engagement.)

+ What are your initial thoughts when you
  hear the word wait?

CHAPTER 1:
Do Something... Anything!

Story Lines

Contrary to what the world may insinuate when they refer to one's spouse as their "other half," God did not make you half a person. You are a complete person with thoughts and dreams and your own, unique personality. And until you know who you are and what you want in life, I don't believe you are ready to look for someone who will live out those dreams alongside you.

Word Search

"Not that I have already obtained all this, or have already been made perfect, but I press on to take hold of that for which Christ Jesus took hold of me. Brothers, I do not consider myself yet to have taken hold of it. But one thing I do: Forgetting what is behind and straining toward what is ahead, I press on toward the goal to win the prize for which God has called me heavenward in Christ Jesus."

~Philippians 3:12-14

Writing Your Story

✦ Do you ever find yourself so focused on "one space" that you fail to see all the other available opportunities awaiting you? What usually occupies your "one space"?

+ Thirteen-year-old Ariel knew her passion for dance had a purpose. Are there areas in your life that you realize you could be using for God? What's keeping you from doing so?

+ Have you ever experienced "shifting" dreams? How do you find yourself reacting when God chooses to turn the path of your journey?

+ Do you often find yourself doing nothing, yet expecting something to happen? List some steps you can begin taking to break free of this apathy.

+ What do you do when you are feeling lonely or "left behind"? Are you prone to drown your sorrows in a quart of Death by Chocolate, or are you more likely to call some friends and have fun without a "significant other"?

Bonus Activity: Awhile back, there was a note bouncing around facebook that challenged people to share 50 random facts about themselves. Do you even know 50 facts about yourself? Today's a great day to find out. Take this challenge to determine what things shape your life and are "list-worthy." Then invite God to mold these 50 things that are very much a part of who you are and who you are yet to become.

CHAPTER 2:
Don't Slow Down; Make Him Catch Up

Story Lines

It's true that Prince C. may be the fulfillment of one dream, but I'm pretty sure you have other dreams as well. I know I do. Let me share something with you that will totally rock your fairytale-founded world: Your dreams are not meant for someone else to fulfill. If God had wanted someone else to write the book He has placed on your heart, play the music that flows from your fingertips, or teach those little second graders whom you have come to adore, He would have given those dreams to someone else. He would have given them to the person who was meant to fulfill them. The fact is, He did. You, my friend, are the only person who can accomplish those dreams, because you are the only one who has dared to dream them.

Word Search

"I will instruct you and teach you in the way you should go; I will counsel you and watch over you. Do not be like the horse or the mule, which have no understanding but must be controlled by bit and bridle or they will not come to you."

~Psalm 32:8-9

Writing Your Story

✦ Is it easy for you to believe that God is

right there with you in every moment? Why or why not?

✦ Do you find yourself able to yield easily to God's instruction, or are you more like a "stubborn mule" which has to be coaxed and prodded before giving in to His ways?

✦ As in the pencil illustration that Donald shared, do you ever find yourself veering from your convictions or dreams in order to search for Mr. Right? What are some ways you can adjust your course settings to begin moving forward along the path of God's plan for your life?

✦ Do you ever find yourself looking at the fairytale backwards—convincing yourself that life doesn't begin until after Prince Charming enters the picture? If so, why do you hold this view? If not, how are you pursuing your dreams at this moment in time?

✦ If Satan is out to destroy dreams and relationships, what do you believe is God's desire for them? How can you actively help build relationships while pursuing your dreams?

CHAPTER 3:
Stop Searching, Sweetheart; Your Prince Is Here

Story Lines

Don't allow yourself to stay so filled with the world's counterfeit dreams that you have no room for Him (Jesus) to come and sweep you into His dance.

Word Search

"Then you will call upon me and come and pray to me, and I will listen to you. You will seek me and find me when you seek me with all your heart."

~Jeremiah 29:12-13

Writing Your Story

✦ Do you ever feel that you are caught up in this chapter's definition of wait (to be hoping for something or on the lookout for something)?

✦ Have you found yourself chasing after human relationships with a passion God intended for you to give to Him?

✦ The word "seek" found in Jeremiah 29:13 suggests the pursuit of a desired objective. It also implies an intensity that borders on desperation. How desperate are you to find your true Prince?

✦ Have you ever considered that maybe it's not so much that others are trying to cram God into your "guy-hole" as it is that you are trying to cram a guy into your "God-hole"? How can you adjust your thinking in this area?

✦ Have you ever experienced moments when Jesus was "overwhelmingly, wonderfully, powerfully, inexplicably, you-wouldn't-believe-it real?" Record your thoughts.

You are Christ's first love, but is He yours? If you have not experienced the joy of knowing that Jesus is your Savior and Lord, today is the perfect day to accept His invitation to life. *(See "The Invitation" found on page 161.)*

CHAPTER 4:
The Things Only God Knows

Story Lines

One day when you look back over the course of your life and see where God has led you, you will be able to say, "Now I get it." Everything will begin to fall into place. Little by little, things will start making sense. Until then, you have to trust that the One who put the envelopes of your life together is only thinking of your best interests.

Word Search

"In my anguish I cried to the Lord, and he answered by setting me free."

~Psalm 118:5

Writing Your Story

✦ Have you ever spent months or even years devoting your efforts and dreams toward someone or something that was not in your best interests? How did you refocus your energies?

✦ Are you tempted to "push the envelope" when it comes to waiting for God to fulfill the desires of your heart? How can you recapture the joy found in the journey along the way?

✦ Can you recall times in your life when God's delay turned out to be a blessing in disguise? Are there prayers you once prayed that you are now thankful were not answered the way you originally desired?

+ Is it hard to place waiting for a husband in the category of a delayed blessing?

+ Has God ever disguised Himself for a season of your life? List some specific instances when God has given you eyes to see Him in unexpected or surprising ways.

CHAPTER 5:
Be Prepared... To Be Used For God's Glory

Story Lines

If one must be ready or available for someone to take or use, I can't think of anyone better to entrust my life to than the One who spoke me into being.

Word Search

"For he (God) chose us in him before the creation of the world to be holy and blameless in his sight. In love he predestined us to be adopted as his sons through Jesus Christ, in accordance with his pleasure and will—to the praise of his glorious grace, which he has freely given us in the One he loves."

~Ephesians 1:4-6

Writing Your Story

✦ Are you prepared to follow God whenever and wherever He calls you to go? If not, why are you hesitating?

✦ Have you ever experienced Jesus "messing up" your carefully-laid plans? How do you handle releasing control of your life during these moments?

✦ Is it hard for you to trust that God has a beautiful ending in store for you? What circumstances in your life, if any, have caused you to doubt His intentions toward you?

✦ *We are still clinging to the way things were before we gave God all that we are.* Is there something you are withholding from the One who gave you everything? Record your thoughts and ask God to help you release these things to Him.

✦ In what areas of your life has your light grown dim? Are you prepared to let the light of Jesus shine through your life in bigger and brighter ways?

CHAPTER 6:
Single By Choice

Story Lines
Instead of searching for a fallible human being in whom you can confide your hopes and dreams, try talking them over with the One who breathed them into being. Let Jesus take you away from the rest of the world for a time, and allow Him to tell you who you were created to be. Invite Him to show you how you were meant to live. Let Him whisper in your ear and tell you who you really are.

Word Search
"I will betroth you to me forever; I will betroth you in righteousness and justice, in love and compassion. I will betroth you in faithfulness, and you will acknowledge the Lord."

~Hosea 2:19-20

Writing Your Story

+ Why are you single? Do you find joy in your singleness?

+ Do you ever find yourself feeling misunderstood in your relationships? Does this make you want to bend your convictions in order to be more fully accepted?

+ How do you normally react to "single-haters"? Is this an area in which you need to deal more graciously?

✦ What are your thoughts regarding "casual dating"? Have you or others been hurt by a casual approach to relationships? Express your thoughts here.

✦ What do you hope to gain by truly setting aside time for Jesus to become your first and forever love?

CHAPTER 7:
Start A Revolution: Learn To Love

Story Lines

"For God so loved the world that he gave his only begotten Son, that whoever believes in him shall not perish but have eternal life." ~John 3:16

I know, I know, you've heard that verse a thousand times. You probably repeated it verbatim with me. But have you ever truly thought about what it means? Have you ever really considered the implications that verse contains? God loved, God gave, and Jesus died. Love—true love—is sacrifice.

Word Search

"'The most important one,' answered Jesus, 'is this: "Hear, O Israel, the Lord our God, the Lord is one. Love the Lord your God with all your heart and with all your soul and with all your mind and with all your strength." The second is this: "Love your neighbor as yourself." There is no commandment greater than these.'"

~ Mark 12:29-31

Writing Your Story

✦ What does true love look like to you? Who portrays this in your life?

✦ Have you ever experienced a relationship with someone where you found yourself wondering if it was really worth it to love? How did this relationship affect how you respond to and approach others?

✦ Do you have a hard time loving others unconditionally or find yourself putting stipulations on your relationships? List some ways you can start broadening the borders and the depths of your love for others today.

✦ While we do not have to be appreciated to love, it sure makes it easier. What are some ways that you can show appreciation to others?

✦ Do you find that you struggle more in giving or in receiving love? Why do you think that is, and how can you grow in this area?

CHAPTER 8:
The Search For Significance

Story Lines

I don't care what you've been told, your life is of value. Regardless of what you've been made to falsely believe, you were created for a purpose. If you've been called ugly, stupid, worthless, or anything else of the like, it's a lie from the pit of hell. God doesn't make mistakes; He creates masterpieces. The first step in embracing your significance is releasing the lies you've carried far too long.

Word Search

"And I pray that you, being rooted and established in love, may have power, together with all the saints, to grasp how wide and long and high and deep is the love of Christ, and to know this love that surpasses knowledge—that you may be filled to the measure of all the fullness of God."

~Ephesians 3:17b-19

Writing Your Story

✦ What lies do you need to cast before the feet of Jesus in order to free yourself to embrace your significance?

✦ Do you have a hard time believing that you are beautiful? How can you begin applying God's truth to your life in this area?

182

Beyond Waiting

- Have you allowed hardness or bitterness
  to replace the strength that God wants
  you to walk in? List some things that might
  have caused this, then ask God to help
  soften your heart.

- Have you allowed comparisons to others
  to dictate how you view yourself? Record
  your thoughts.

- How does it make you feel to know that
  you are irrevocably and unconditionally
  loved by the God of the universe?

Acknowledgments

First and foremost, I have to give glory to the God who argued me into writing this book. All right, You win. So I'm more than just a storyteller. Thanks for always being so persistent and moving me to places beyond my wildest dreams.

An unimaginable amount of thanks belongs to Barbara Snyder: the best mother, friend, editor, and sounding board that could ever grace this girl's life. Thanks for spending hours of your life creating this book with me, Bud, and uh… what was the rest? Okay, so the truth is that your name should be on the cover right next to mine. I honestly could not have done this without you. Thanks for always encouraging the one dream that truly mattered.

Shannon Primicerio, I'd say you have no idea what your endorsement means to me, but I know that you were in my shoes once upon a time. Thanks for paying it forward.

Amy and Donna McAllister, thanks for your feedback on the first draft. I love you for so much more than your editing skills.

Virginia Tobias, thank you for catching those last few mistakes and reminding me that Beyond Waiting is a timeless tale for young and old alike.

Jasmine Elm, our photo shoot made me feel like an official author. (Not to mention, the results were amazing.) Thanks for dreaming with me.

Speaking of photo shoots, I really must thank Sarah Tichenor and Lachlan Earles for risking life and limb to recreate the cover image I had envisioned in my mind. I'm sorry it didn't work out, but I'm still incredibly thankful to have friends like you who will go above and beyond to help make my dreams come true.

Heather Kirk, it's amazing how you took a black-and-white manuscript and turned it into a work of art. Thank you for all your feedback, suggestions, and hard work. I love the outcome.

Cheri Thompson, I think you've been involved in every graphics project I've ever dealt with in my life. I'm so glad you could be a part of this one, too. Thank you for seeing what I couldn't see and for taking that vision and running with it.

Thank you, Mom, John, Lynn, Amber, Amy, Katie, Mindy, Trisha, Gary, and anyone else I may have forced to suffer through an endless list of terrible suggestions for a subtitle—especially Dad and Dave, who kept my heart light in the midst of it. Sorry the pop-up pictures didn't work out. Maybe next time.

And to all of the people whose words and stories sprinkle the pages of this manuscript... This book, much like my life, would not be complete without each of you.